PRACTICAL SHIP-HANDLING

BY

MALCOLM C. ARMSTRONG

Pilot

"Malcolm C. Armstrong is also the author of *Pilot Ladder Safety* published by International Maritime Press, 78 John Street, Woollahra, N.S.W. 2025, Australia."

GLASGOW
BROWN, SON & FERGUSON, LTD.
52 DARNLEY STREET, G41 2SG

First Edition   1980

ISBN 0 85174 387 0
© 1980 BROWN, SON & FERGUSON, LIMITED, GLASGOW, G41 2SG
Printed and Made in Great Britain

CONTENTS

CONTENTS

LIST OF ILLUSTRATIONS

FOREWORD

Ship handling is an art and as the artist must learn to use and to appreciate the materials available to him, so must the ship handler have a complete understanding of the materials of his craft. It is only a thorough understanding of them, their abilities and their limitations which can enable him to take his ship (be it a small coaster or a VLCC) to and from its berth with precision, safety and efficiency.

Little opportunity is available for ships' officers or even for shipmasters in the general pattern of world shipping today, to gain any experience of the manoeuvring of their ships in narrow waters, into and out of port, or to understand and appreciate the factors governing these manoeuvres. This book aims to fill that gap.

The author, Captain Malcolm Armstrong, has a depth of background and knowledge to draw upon. Having progressed through the stages from apprentice to master, he joined the New South Wales pilot service in 1966. His deep interest in his profession led him to being elected Australian pilots' representative and Vice President of the International Maritime Pilots' Association. As a pilot in the ports of Sydney and Botany Bay he is handling day and night many of the world's largest passenger vessels, container ships, deep draughted tankers and bulk carriers in addition to the more prosaic cargo ships.

After a career spanning three years in command in the Australian and Pacific Islands trade, twenty-nine years as Pilot and Senior Pilot in Sydney and Botany Bay, followed by five years as Harbour Master/Pilot in Solomon Islands, I read the manuscript of this book with a highly critical eye. It is an admirable work and the Author is to be congratulated. His book deserves a place on every navigator's bookshelf.

PHILIP LUSHER

Sydney, New South Wales
April 1980.

PREFACE

A few days after taking up my first command, I had my first experience as a ship-handler. It was a small ship, although I did not think so at the time. A lot of water has gone under bridges since then. The proficiency gained from handling a wide variety of ships on three thousand occasions in four quite different ports, must now give me an advantage over a first trip master.

Technique and ability develop with practice, but it is also necessary to have knowledge. A career at sea gave me the opportunity to become a pilot, but a book such as this one would have enabled me to be much better prepared for my first tentative experiments in the art of ship-handling. If I had had ready access to the same information and advice a few years earlier I would have been a far more helpful officer in pilotage waters.

INTRODUCTION

Ship-handling is an acquired art, practised by harbour pilots. Masters and officers of large ships seldom have the opportunity or the necessity to handle their own ships in confined waters. However it is necessary for ships' officers to gain some knowledge of ship-handling as part of their career training and in order to give intelligent and correct answers to examination questions on the subject.

It is important that ships' officers and others who assist the pilot, should be given some guidance on procedures in pilotage waters in order to produce a team effort that will ensure the safe and efficient handling of a ship.

Much piloting is similar to the navigation and chart work practised by ships' officers in coastal waters. The application of a pilot's essential local knowledge to this navigation cannot be generalised. However there are certain fundamentals that can be explained in connection with practical ship-handling and there are principles, rules and theories that must be observed and understood.

Ships have changed over the years and ship-handling has to be adapted to these changes. The average size of ship has increased, but ports have not always increased in size accordingly. At one time the only large ships were passenger liners and even though they were safely handled with primitive communications and very limited tug assistance, they were better manned and more powerfully engined than many modern monsters of the deep. Also, ships' hull plating is not as strong or as thick as it used to be!

Large container ships with towering deck cargo cannot be treated the same way as small general cargo ships. Car carriers and mammoth tankers require special attention. Much of the former charm and likeable character of ships is missing; but to a pilot, every new floating object presents a challenge.

THE NAVIGATORS

The Pilot

The pilot is engaged as an expert. He knows the harbour and he is a skilful ship-handler. He is a seaman who specialises in this particular work. His guiding principle is safety. In many areas pilotage is compulsory; the master must engage a pilot and must allow the pilot to handle his ship; this is the law. The master may have a knowledge of the port or it may be his first visit; the pilot's job is still the same in either case.

The pilot is adaptable; some ships he handles frequently and others he sees only once in a lifetime.

The master may have handled his own ship on certain occasions and he may be a very competent ship-handler; however, this does not alter the pilot's position on the ship. The pilot must take the ship from beginning to end of the pilotage.

The pilot's job is always the same, and yet it is always different. There are many variables including wind, tide, visibility and draught. Even the same ship into the same berth behaves differently every time. One pilot will handle a ship slightly differently from the way it is done by another. The attitude and assistance of master, officers and crew also influence the pilotage operation.

It has been said that reliability is the cardinal quality a pilot must possess. Ships' officers and masters have to rely upon a pilot to deliver them safely to the pilotage destination. Often a master is entering the port for the first time; he may not even have a chart of the area; he is entirely in the hands of the pilot.

The pilot's task is made easier or more difficult by the

action of the master. If the master is familiar with the port, he must still allow the pilot to continue in his own way without interference. A master who knows his own ship may think he is better able to handle the ship than a pilot; but unfamiliarity with a particular ship is not a handicap to an experienced pilot.

A pilot does not want to compete with the master for the control of the ship; but in order to maintain effective control he must be able to orchestrate all the forces at his disposal. Ship-handling is an intellectual exercise as well as being practical. The pilot is always assessing the situation and thinking ahead to his next order; he does not want his concentration or judgment interrupted.

The Officer of the Watch

The master usually takes over from the officer of the watch prior to arrival in pilotage waters, but the officer still has important functions to perform.

When the pilot is on board and actually conducting the ship, the master and officers must still bear their share of work and responsibility for the safety of the ship; they should not simply depart from the bridge and leave the pilot without assistance.

Shipowners usually impress upon masters and officers that their responsibilities do not end when the pilot comes on board; but officers should not be misled by the archaic log entry "helm and engines to master's orders and pilot's advice". The pilot (with exceptions in some non-compulsory areas) is in charge of the pilotage. He has the "conduct" of the ship. The ship is not being navigated under his advice. There have been accidents for which the pilot has been found to blame and the master exonerated. There will always be accidents as long as there are ships, but it is unrealistic to think that all the responsibility is on the master and none on the pilot.

The Inter-Governmental Maritime Consultative Organisation (IMCO), on the subject of *Navigation with Pilot Embarked* has said: "If the officer of the watch is in any doubt as to the Pilot's actions or intentions, he should seek clarification from the Pilot and if doubt still exists he should notify the master immediately and take whatever action is necessary before the master arrives".

The last part of this IMCO directive does not entirely meet with the approval of pilots. However, the word "necessary" is most important and could be the crux of the whole statement. In the confines of a harbour which is the situation that this book is dealing with, the master is usually on the bridge. The mind boggles at the thought of an inexperienced and perhaps unqualified officer taking the ship out of the pilot's hands.

The officer of the watch is not expected to have the knowledge of a pilot, but he should do his best to gain an understanding of what is going on. Ships do not just come and go of their own volition, they must be handled with personal care.

An officer's part in pilotage commences before the ship arrives at the pilot station. From charts, publications, VHF, radio messages etc. he should find out where the pilot is to be picked up, what procedure is required for that operation, and he should ensure that boarding facilities are checked and prepared in good time. These are all the responsibility of the master but require an officer's supervision. Bridge equipment must be tested. If possible, bridge windows should be cleaned to improve visibility.

An information sheet should be available to the pilot. This information will include the ship's dimensions, tonnages, draught, particulars of engines, thrusters, harbour speeds and any special peculiarities that affect the ship's manoeuvrability.

Although, in a sense, a pilot is a one man band, the degree of efficiency and safety and the end result of his work depend largely upon a team effort. The bridge officer plays an important role.

A pilot should give orders clearly and loud enough to be heard by the master and the officer. The officer must repeat the order. When operating the engine control or telegraph, the officer must always check the revolution or pitch indicators to see that the correct movement has resulted from his execution of the order. Any incorrect response should be immediately reported to the master and the pilot. If the engines are inadvertently started in the wrong direction, the bridge tele- graph should be changed to the "Stop" position, and then the original order can be repeated.

Helm orders may be given directly to the man at the wheel or it may be necessary to pass them by intercommunication from bridge wing to wheelhouse. They may have to be translated. A pilot will usually confine his orders to degrees of rudder, port and starboard or left and right. Imprecise orders are not easily understood and may be misinterpreted by the man at the wheel. The officer should always check that the man at the wheel executes the order correctly and he must immediately rectify and report any mistake. Not all ships are adequately fitted with indicators and the pilot and master may not be aware of the wheel going the wrong way until after a vital time lapse.

The officer must be sure that the man at the wheel is competent and sober. It is quite in order to have a trainee quartermaster or cadet on the wheel, but there should be an experienced helmsman at hand to take over if necessary and to assist the trainee. If the wheel is relieved during a pilotage, the officer on duty should make sure that the helmsman reports to master and pilot the present course or wheel position.

There will be messages on VHF from other ships and from the port operations centre. The officer must keep a listening watch for these. When the pilot is outside the wheelhouse he may not hear the radio and he will depend on the officer to keep him informed.

Orders and messages have to be sent to and from the forward and aft ends of the ship, in connection with berthing, anchoring, securing tugs etc. These messages must be passed accurately.

It is helpful, especially on a large bridge, if the officer follows the pilot like an unobtrusive shadow. It is frustrating to be left alone in the wing of the bridge if there is no one within earshot. It is also helpful to have an officer permanently at the engine telegraph. If there is only one officer available he has to be everywhere at the same time.

Another duty of the officer on the bridge is to keep a careful note of times. Times to be recorded include engine movements, the securing of tugs, singling up, letting go or sending away mooring lines, anchoring, and any other significant incidents relating to the ship's progress. On many ships it is normal to plot the ship's position on the chart in harbour limits. This is a good practice and useful experience but it cannot be done if only one officer is available. On some ships a commentary of the pilotage is tape recorded.

In accordance with the International Collision Regulations, a proper look-out must be maintained at all times. The radar should be operating in pilotage waters. In congested waters, the officer will need to use common sense and discretion when reporting other craft.

Look-out is not confined to the water. An officer must be constantly on the alert within the bridge for any malfunction of equipment, particularly the gyro compass. Ships' bridges have a plethora of instruments, consoles, dials, switches, lights and alarms. Many of these have no connection with navigation. An alarm buzzer sounding at a critical stage of a manoeuvre can be most disconcerning to a pilot. The officer must immediately advise the pilot whether there is anything wrong, and should reassure him if the signal is irrelevant to his handling of the ship. The pilot and the ship's officers do not always share the same native language and a pilot should not be kept uninformed while a long telephone conversation takes place in response to the indication of a possibly serious malfunction.

An efficient bridge officer should be the pilot's right hand man (or woman).

The Master

It is not the purpose of this book to teach a master his business. The book is intended to assist in the education, training and qualification of ships' officers. The following comments are therefore to advise officers how they should one day conduct themselves in pilotage waters in order to assist in the performance of safe ship-handling.

The master, of course, remains in command of the ship when a pilot is on board. A master's duties are many and varied. Entering and leaving port occupies only part of his time, and only part of his overall responsibilities. However, the safety of the ship is most at risk, and consequently pressure on the master is at a peak when manoeuvring in the confines of a harbour. It makes sense to engage a specialist—a pilot—to care for the ship in pilotage waters. A master may be only too pleased to hand over to the pilot; or he may want to feel that he is still doing the job himself, even though he is not. The relationship between master and pilot has always been a delicate one; it must be one of mutual trust and respect. The practical reality of the situation is that the master remains in charge of the ship and the pilot is in charge of handling the ship. An analogous situation arises when a surgeon performs an operation; the patient remains in command of his body but engages the surgeon to take charge of the operation (without interference!).

Masters are very possessive about their ships and so they should be; but if the ship "belongs to" the master, it must be remembered that the harbour "belongs to" the pilot. The pilot is responsible not only for the ship he is piloting, but also for other ships, tugs and various craft that may be encountered or used; and for wharves, locks, docks, bridges and shore installations; and he has a responsibility to the local community.

Some ships are so undermanned that the only people on the bridge with the pilot are the master and the man at the wheel. In these circumstances the master is a very busy man indeed and he has to perform the duties already described as being functions of the officer of the watch.

The master will naturally listen carefully to every order that is given by the pilot. He will closely watch the manoeuvre. He should not interfere or give conflicting orders, but should see that the pilot's orders are properly followed. If the pilot asks for half ahead he does not want dead slow and if he asks for slow astern he does not want full astern; he needs to know what power he still has available. The master should make sure that the pilot is aware of what speed to expect from the various engine settings.

The master may want to be given in advance an outline of the proposed manoeuvre or berthing operation. This is a reasonable request but it is not always possible for the pilot to give a satisfying answer. A pilot must be flexible and will change his intentions to suit circumstances that arise.

A master often thinks a pilot is going too fast or getting too close. He may be right about the speed, but the ship must eventually be brought close to the wharf. Pilots are at home in these situations whereas the master may be more at ease on the wide ocean.

Unless the pilot is obviously drunk, ill or behaving recklessly or irresponsibly, the master must restrain himself from interfering. He is always entitled to suggest that the ship is going too fast and a tactful pilot will usually slow down. In most cases the pilot will be well aware of when he should slow down or go astern, and the master may realize afterwards that his suggestion was premature.

The master must see that his officers and crew are at their stations in plenty of time and are well primed in their duties. The bridge officers' functions have been outlined. The officers at each end of the ship must maintain communications with the bridge; if possible they should watch the bridge for visual communication; tugs have to be secured exactly in the manner that is required; lines run as soon as possible, but not before instructions have been given from the bridge. On departure, lines must be taken in promptly and reported when clear. The officer aft should be conscious of the fact that those on the bridge are waiting to hear that the propeller is clear. When the ship has headway, the stern lines may trail safely clear, long before they are out of the water. A pilot is always aware of the consequences of a fouled propeller, but it is sometimes necessary to go ahead on the engines as soon as a line is trailing.

Officers should be encouraged by the master to offer

information regarding distances off the wharf and other ships when swinging or berthing. The pilot knows that in most instances these messages will be inaccurate, because estimation of distances is difficult and much practice is required. Most officers will underestimate the distance, but this is better than sending no information at all. It is quite possible that 100 metres will be called as 50 metres, and this may cause consternation among master and officers on the bridge, but as the distance closes, estimates will gradually improve.

When a ship is entering the channel on departure from a berth, the officer at the bow or stern should call the bridge and advise of any harbour traffic in sight.

Before going forward or aft on arrival or departure, officers should report to the bridge for any special instructions from the pilot or the master. This may save unnecessary communications and time-wasting later.

The master should tell the pilot of any particulars that may affect the handling of the ship. For example, if only one boiler is operating instead of two; or any other limitation imposed on the engine power; or any history of engine or windlass failures; or shortage of crew for mooring.

The pilot will have started his assessment of the ship before he came on board and he will soon find out for himself how she behaves. Every manoeuvre is different and cannot be exactly predicted in advance, but it is helpful to have some basic information available on the bridge regarding the ship's manoeuvring characteristics.

THE SHIP

There are three characteristics which give a pilot his first impression of a ship: its size; its general appearance or design; and the type of propulsion.

Size

The larger the ship, the more demanding the job will be. Large ships are intended for long ocean passages; they are designed to keep going forward, not to stop. Engine power does not increase in proportion to increases in ship size. A 50,000 tonnes ship does not require twice the power of a 25,000 tonnes ship to be driven forward at the same speed; but the larger ship will be more difficult to stop, and this is the first problem with which a ship-handler has to contend. A large ship that is fast and powerful may be able to stop in the same number of ship-lengths as a smaller ship, but the actual distance will be much greater. If a large ship is underpowered, this problem is worse. In order to stop within a reasonable distance it is necessary to go more slowly; but when speed is reduced, steering is less effective.

It is more difficult to judge speed from the high bridge of a large ship. When swinging off a berth, extra length of ship requires more swinging room, and estimation of distance from the wharf becomes more difficult. In the event of failure of telephone or walkie-talkie, the bridge is isolated from a distant forecastle or poop.

If a ship comes alongside a wharf sufficiently heavily to cause damage, a large ship will cause more damage than a small ship at the same velocity.

The larger the area of ship that is exposed to the wind, the

11

more difficult it is to control the ship. A long ship may have part of its length in the lee of a wharf, and the other end of the ship feeling the full force of a very strong wind. Similarly, when passing or rounding a point of land within the harbour, one end of the ship may be set strongly by the current, while the other end is in still water. This is not such a problem in a small ship because less time is taken to clear the point of land or the end of the wharf. When handling large ships it is virtually essential to have tug assistance.

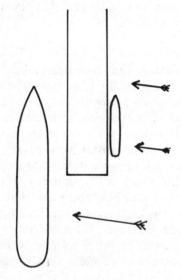

Fig. 1—*Part of ship in a lee, part exposed.*

What is a large ship? VLCCs (Very Large Crude Carriers) speak for themselves and make other ships look small by comparison. A 20,000 tonnes ship was once considered very large. In 1952, the biggest tanker on order anywhere in the world was 45,000 deadweight tons. These are still large ships—they can only be considered small when compared with ships that are several times their size. Length is some-times a more relevant criterion than tonnage. It is fairly safe to say that a vessel under 100 metres in length is a small ship, over 200 metres is large and anything in between can be called large or small.

The relative size of a ship compared with the space in which it must be manoeuvred is relevant to the degree of difficulty encountered. A ship of 5000 tonnes may be large for a port that normally handles ships of 500 tonnes. However, irrespective of the manoeuvre, a ship of 5000 tonnes does not present the same problems of dimensions, mass, inertia and momentum as a ship of 50,000 tonnes. A very late decision when handling a small ship may avert an accident, but the same decision at the same time in a large ship may be too late.

Design

There was a time when ships came into one of three categories, viz. bridge forward, bridge amidships, or bridge aft. This is still so, up to a point, but there are other factors which are more important than the longitudinal siting of the bridge and which negate the advantages and disadvantages associated with these three bridge positions.

Bridge aft

Most pilots prefer the bridge aft. When looking ahead, practically all of the ship can be seen. It is not necessary to be continually looking aft to see if the stern is clear, and when one does look aft it is easier to assess clearance because not much of the ship is there.

Rate of swing and the commencement and end of swing are more easily judged.

There are disadvantages in being a long way from the forecastle head. Selecting a precise spot for anchoring requires careful allowance for speed and distance. Visual communication is not possible. Launches, ferries, yachts and other small harbour craft become lost from view. The practice of watching the angle on the bow of crossing vessels has very limited value; it may be possible to judge that the other vessel will not collide with the bridge, but there may still be a collision course with the foredeck. In fog, the extra length forward may be sufficient to prevent the sighting from the bridge of anything ahead of the ship.

Bridge forward

Some of the advantages of bridge forward are dis-advantages of bridge aft, and vice versa. The pilot has an excellent view of the berth when making a head-on approach or when swinging bow to the wharf. He can almost look down the hawse pipe when anchoring. He gains valuable metres of visibility in fog. When entering locks or dry dock it is useful to be at the end that arrives first, in order to have a close up view of entry and for visual communication with the shore.

Disadvantages of bridge forward include the difficulty in assessing a true sense of the ship's heading without standing amidships or looking aft. Viewed from the wing of the bridge, objects on one bow may appear to be on the other.

Swinging without headway is the same whether the bridge is right forward or right aft, but rounding close to a point of land in the harbour through a turn of about 90 degrees requires quite different judgment and adaptability.

Bridge amidships

The main advantage of this position is that the ship-handler is at or near the pivoting point of the ship when swinging. It is the best position in a small ship, especially if the forecastle and poop are both visible from the bridge. Visual communication is very important in small ships where things happen fast in comparison with the ponderous manoeuvres of large ships.

An amidships bridge in a large ship affords a good indication of rate of swing when looking forward or aft, but on the other hand, each end is distant and requires equal attention.

The siting of the bridge influences the manner in which a ship will be affected by the wind. There is no advantageous or disadvantageous position from this point of view, but it is a factor of which the ship-handler must be aware. Ships are not so predictable that it can be said with certainty that the end of the ship to catch most wind is the end with the bridge housing. A high superstructure on an otherwise clear deck will provide wind resistance at that point, but this may be offset by other deck houses or deck cargo. If a ship has a very light draught forward and is deep in the water aft, the wind may have a stronger influence on the bow than on the stern, even if the bridge is aft.

Container ships

Most container ships have the bridge aft, or at least well abaft the midship point. A well designed container ship has a very high bridge so that it is possible to see the water as close as possible ahead of the ship. Not all container ships are well designed in this respect and some were not designed to be container ships at all. The expression "loaded to the gunwales" is no longer applicable; the sky is the limit. Containers are sometimes stacked so high that it is not possible to see ahead over the top. On ocean passages this is bad enough, but

Fig. 2—*Visibility restricted by high deck cargo.*

Fig. 3—*Visibility improved by stepping down deck cargo.*

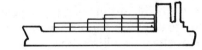

Fig. 4—*Container ship with a high bridge.*

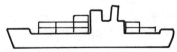

Fig. 5—*Containers stepped down forward and aft.*

inside harbour it is most hazardous. Judgment of distances becomes more difficult; other craft disappear from view miles away, or may not be seen at all. When the bridge of a ship is low, the deck cargo should also be kept low and should be stepped down if necessary towards the ends of the ship—especially towards the forward end.

Many "conventional" general cargo ships and bulk car-riers have been adapted for the carriage of containers. This adaptation is in the form of fittings in holds and on hatch covers to facilitate stowage and securing of containers. The ship becomes a more efficient cargo carrier, but more of a headache to the pilot because of lost visibility and additional area of windage. A ship with bridge amidships may be so laden that visibility is restricted ahead and astern.

Car carriers

These are among the worst ships to handle, and they are surely the most grotesque. They vary in dimensions from very small to the size of a large passenger liner. In appearance they resemble a floating shoe box. They are high sided and catch more wind than container ships or passenger ships, but they usually have less power than any of these.

A full load represents very little deadweight, consequently car carriers are never deep in the water and this aggravates the influence of wind. Without tug assistance they may be practi-cally unmanageable and yet often they are not fitted with suitable bollards for the securing of tugs.

Floating car parks are a headache for pilots and masters even when they do not have all the faults mentioned here.

Figure No. 6 shows the outline of a typical car carrier. The bridge is like a match box on top of a shoe box and is back from the forward edge. Looking ahead from the bridge, visibility is seriously impaired by the deck which extends from side to side and well forward. It is not possible to see the forecastle or to see water or wharves close by on either side of the ship. The advantages of a forward sited bridge are nullified. Looking aft, there are ventilators and deck houses which obstruct the view. In order to see clearly ahead or astern it is necessary to go to the extreme wing of the bridge, and then everything is obscured on the other side.

If the bridge were raised one or two decks higher (see Fig. 7), visibility would be much better and ship-handling much safer.

Another type of car carrier is the converted bulk carrier. A large box is placed on the foredeck. The original bridge is left in place, aft, but is not used (see Fig. 8). A new bridge is added

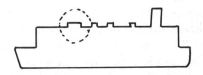

Fig. 6—*Badly sighted bridge, poor visibility.*

Fig. 7—*Visibility improved by raising the bridge.*

Fig. 8—*Converted bulk carrier with new bridge.*

on top of the cargo space, and the same problems of visibility arise that have just been described. Bulk carriers are not usually the most powerful ships and the additional high freeboard makes them even less manageable in strong wind conditions.

If ships are built or converted without sufficient regard to their safe manoeuvrability, it must be expected that restrictions will be placed on them. Possibly they will be only handled in daylight hours, or they may be restricted to certain berths, or not allowed to move if the wind is too strong. Pilots do not like placing limitations on ships, and a difficult job is always a challenge, but safety must be the first consideration—not only the safety of the ship to be handled, but the safety of the port.

Passenger ships

These come into a category of their own, whether they are large or small. To an experienced pilot they are among the best ships to handle. They are usually efficiently run with a sufficient number of qualified officers on the bridge to ensure a quick response to orders and a careful monitoring of all movements. There is plenty of engine power because the ships are built for high speed operation; usually twin screws which are an advantage in large ships and in small powerful ships. There is no shortage of crew for mooring. Bridge equipment, communications and mooring lines are kept in good condition.

MACHINERY AND PROPULSION

The propeller

The purpose of a propeller is to work its way through the water, the same way that a corkscrew goes into a cork. In so doing it pushes the ship ahead. A propeller (with a fixed pitch) is designed for maximum efficiency when going ahead, therefore it cannot pull the ship astern as well or as quickly, as it can push. The number of blades on a propeller varies according to the whim, or knowledge, of the designer, and the effectiveness of propellers also varies; but the ship-handler does not take this into account until he feels for himself what response he is getting in the particular circumstances of the manoeuvre. The effectiveness of the propulsion also depends to some extent on the shape of the hull. As a ship moves forward, water has to fill the space that was occupied by the ship; if this space were not filled, the propeller would have no water in which to operate; therefore the hull must be shaped to allow a good flow of water towards the propeller, otherwise efficiency will be lost.

The terms "right handed" and "left handed" refer to the direction of rotation of the propeller when going ahead facing forward. They mean clockwise and anti-clockwise rotation respectively. Single screw ships with a fixed pitch propeller are nearly always right handed. Controllable pitch propellers are usually left handed.

When engines are put astern, the propeller exerts a transverse thrust on the stern of the ship. A right handed propeller can be expected to move the stern to port when going astern. The stern is said to "cut" to port.

The transverse thrust is most apparent when the ship is at

a very light draught with part of the propeller out of the water. The propeller behaves like a paddle wheel driving the stern sideways. If the propeller is rotating close to the surface, air is drawn in making the water less dense and less resistant around the upper part of the propeller than at the lowest point of rotation. When the propeller is deep in the water, the transverse thrust may not be noticeable.

This oversimplifies the matter. In actual fact there are a number of forces at work in the turbulent water surrounding a propeller, and some of these tend to move the ship against the usual "cut"; but as a rule the resultant transverse thrust is in the direction stated here, and the paddle wheel action is the most easily remembered explanation.

Unless the propeller is well out of the water, the transverse thrust is not usually significant with an ahead movement except at the initial take off from rest. Unlike an astern movement, an ahead movement can be controlled by use of the rudder.

Fig. 9—*Paddle wheel effect.*

Steam ships and motor ships

At one time, the pilot's favourite was the steam reciprocating engine. It was reliable, it would turn over at any desired speed, gave almost instant response from ahead to astern and was no trouble to start or stop. This engine is now a rarity and ship-handling has become more difficult with its passing.

Other types of machinery well suited to ship-handling are turbo electric and diesel electric. The propeller shaft is driven by an electric motor and can be stopped and reversed very quickly. These are often fitted to ferries which are in and out of port every few hours, but they are seldom encountered elsewhere.

The most common machinery is the diesel engine driving a fixed pitch propeller. A ship with this type of propulsion is given the prefix "m.v." or "m.s." for motor vessel or motor ship, or sometimes "m.t." for motor tanker. The second most common propulsion is steam turbine; the ship is usually given the simple prefix "s.s." and is known as a turbine ship.

From the ship-handler's point of view, a motor ship is preferable to a turbine ship. A diesel engine can be instantly stopped and can usually be quickly reversed (some more quickly than others). When the engines are used to take way off the ship they can be stopped at the moment way is lost and propulsion then ceases immediately; whereas a turbine continues to turn for some time after it has been "stopped". So it is necessary to order "stop" with a turbine when the ship still has way on, or else be prepared to travel some distance in the opposite direction.

Diesel engines can be quickly accelerated and this is useful when emergency power is required, or when a short burst of power is needed to assist with a turn. Turbines increase and decrease speed more slowly.

A very important disadvantage with a turbine ship is that stern power is only 40%–50% of ahead power. This is because a smaller, separate, turbine is used for astern movements. Older turbines are notorious for their lack of stern power. It is not a problem in a very powerful ship because there is still plenty of stern power for stopping, provided headway is kept within reasonable bounds.

It is quite common for turbines to keep turning slowly ahead when supposed to be stopped. This could be a serious problem if the ship-handler were not aware of it, but it can also be used to advantage as a very slow "Dead Slow" in the final approach to the berth or when requiring bare steerage way in the channel.

There are disadvantages with diesel engines. Some cannot run slowly and a powerful motor ship may have a "Dead Slow" of 9 or 10 knots which necessitates repeatedly stopping and restarting the engines to keep speed down. It is not always possible to get an immediate astern movement if the ship is moving fast through the water.

Diesel engines are started by forcing compressed air into the cylinders. The supply of air has been known to be used up and consequently no more engine movements are available until the compressor has replenished the supply. This was quite common in early motor ships but not in modern ships. If there is likely to be such a problem, the engineers should, if possible, give adequate warning of the number of starts that are still available so that the pilot can conduct his manoeuvre accordingly.

Controllable pitch propellers

The foregoing comments and comparisons of motor ships and steamers refer to ships with conventional propellers. Many ships are fitted with controllable pitch propellers (CPP), sometimes called variable pitch propellers (VPP). In these ships, the engines remain running at constant pre-determined revolutions and the speed of the ship is increased or decreased by adjusting the pitch of the propeller blades. The "Stop" position is achieved by reducing the pitch to nil so that the propeller is still turning but is not gripping the water. The pitch can be varied for astern or ahead movements without reversing the direction in which the propeller is turning.

This system has advantages and disadvantages compared with fixed propeller propulsion.

Speed can be conveniently reduced, either ahead or astern, to a bare minimum; this is useful when positioning the ship the last few centimetres. However, it is difficult to find neutral in the Stop position and slight sternway or headway may result when it is not required.

There is no worry about having to restart the engines. Propeller pitch can be very quickly increased, decreased or reversed.

Steering at slow speeds is less effective with variable pitch propellers than with fixed propellers. When pitch is reduced quickly, e.g. if Dead Slow is applied while the ship is still travelling at Full of Half, steerage may be lost until the ship's speed has dropped to correspond with the engine order. Speed should be reduced gradually. When pitch is in the neutral position the rudder may have no effect whatsoever.

A constantly turning propeller presents some problems. It is a hazard to mooring launches. Extra care is required when running lines or letting go, or if a tug's line carries away. In the latter case the engines can be stopped if necessary, but it is not usual to stop the engines when manoeuvring with a variable pitch propeller, and the unusual always takes a little longer. The officer at the controls should always be prepared for the order to stop the engines—as distinct from "stopping" the pitch. The officer should also be prepared to increase the revolutions if this is required (and if available) in case of emergency. Revolutions used for manoeuvring are usually less than full sea speed so there is something in reserve.

Controllable pitch propellers normally keep turning in the same direction all the time. Some have the means for reversing rotation, but this is unusual. It is important that the ship-handler knows whether the ship is left handed or right handed. The pilot should be given this information on every ship.

There is one serious disadvantage with controllable pitch propellers, from the pilot's point of view, but it does not apply on all ships. This is the type of control and the uncertainty of how much power is being applied at any time. It is most important that there should be pre-arranged pitch settings corresponding to the orders "Full", "Half", "Slow", and "Dead Slow"—ahead and astern. The expected approximate speed at each of these settings should be clearly listed in the wheel house. This information is usually available on a ship with fixed propeller(s) but is often neglected when there is a controllable pitch propeller. If a speed other than those listed is required, it can be requested specifically. The availability of any desired speed is an advantage of the system; but if a pilot orders Half Ahead or Slow Astern or any other standard movement he should know what response he can expect to get—and he should get the same response the next time he gives the same order. Unfortunately, many ships are not fitted with anything resembling the old fashioned engine room telegraph and this has been replaced by a lever which has rather meaningless graduations from, say, 1 to 10. The "Stop" position is not always in the vertical position as it should be for quick reference, but may be at any position. The graduations correspond to angles of pitch, but are only readable by close scrutiny and then require reference to a conversion table. This problem is made more serious by failure to fit adequate pitch indicators. There is often a large revolution indicator which is of little value because the revolutions are kept constant, and a very small pitch indicator which is almost useless because of its size and its lack of information. Some pitch indicators do not show the angle of pitch, but merely an approximation between nil and maximum.

No master or officer would change an engine room telegraph from one position to another without an order from the pilot, or at least, not without consulting or advising the pilot. Some masters take an entirely different attitude when they have a simple pitch control lever; instead of complying with the pilot's orders, they are tempted to give whatever they consider may be required at the time, and they may even make "adjustments" later according to their own assessment of the situation. This is *a most dangerous practice* and ships' officers should be wary of getting into such bad habits. If the master thinks a different engine order is required he may say so to the pilot, but the pilot must know what is going on and must be in charge. If a pilot calls for an increase or decrease in speed and finds that unbeknown to him, the pitch has already been increased or decreased, his control of the manoeuvre has been seriously weakened. The pilot must know at all times how much he is using of his available power resources.

The International Maritime Pilots' Association has issued a Notice on this subject and it is reproduced here in full:

"The International Maritime Pilots' Association (IMPA) is concerned about certain aspects of bridge control, particularly on vessels with controllable pitch propellers.

"Vessels with non-controllable pitch propellers are

normally fitted with an engine room telegraph which clearly indicates Dead Slow, Slow, Half and Full for ahead and astern movements, also Stop which is placed so that the telegraph handle is vertical. Information is usually available on the bridge giving the approximate speed in knots to be expected at each of the (ahead) speed settings. With such equipment and information the pilot can be reasonably sure of what speed he will get when he gives an engine order; he can also expect the speed to remain steady until he gives another order and he can see at a glance the engine setting at any time; this can, of course, be checked by observing the revolution indicator.

"The control lever which has replaced the engine telegraph in many ships with controllable pitch propellers does not give any clear indication of the speed that has been ordered except by close scrutiny followed by com- parison of revolution and pitch indicators. It is not uncommon for the master or ship's officer to make further adjustments to the control lever on his own assessment of the situation without reference to the pilot; this is a dangerous practice because the pilot does not know how much engine power is being transmitted or whether it has been changed since his last order.

"In the interests of safety it is suggested by IMPA that all vessels whether fitted with controllable pitch propellers or not, should have specific settings clearly marked on the telegraph or control lever console showing Dead Slow, Slow, Half and Full (ahead and astern) and that Stop should always be the position in which the lever or telegraph handle is vertical. A table should be compiled on every ship to indicate pre-determined approximate speeds to be expected at these specific engine or pitch settings and during manoeuvres these should be followed as closely as possible. Speeds other than these should only be given when particularly required and ordered."

Twin Screws

Two propellers do not necessarily make a ship more manoeuvrable than a single screw ship. There are certain

c

advantages in having more than one propeller and the most obvious one is that an engine failure does not leave the ship without any propulsion. Twin screws are an advantage in a large ship but not always in a small ship.

In a small ship the propellers are close together and do not give much turning moment when used one ahead, one astern. If the ship is underpowered it is better to have all the power in one propeller to get maximum thrust.

A single rudder is not as effective in a twin screw ship as in a single screw ship; therefore the latter steers better, especially at slow speeds. The effectiveness of a rudder is due to the drag in the water on the side of application, and also the thrust of water from the propeller(s). A rudder that is midway between two propellers, but not in the slip stream of either, is not as effective as a rudder that is immediately behind a single propeller. When engines are stopped, a twin screw ship may steer marginally better than a single screw ship because the rudder is not directly behind the propeller and is therefore less influenced by the disturbed water passing through stationary propeller blades. Twin rudders make a twin screw ship much more manoeuvrable.

An advantage of twin screws in a fast motor ship with high minimum revolutions is that it is possible to proceed at a reasonably slow speed and still retain good steerage, by stopping one engine.

Fixed pitch twin screws usually turn outwards when going ahead; i.e. the starboard one is right handed and the port left handed. This is the most suitable arrangement for manoeuvrability; when one engine is put astern, the turning moment on the ship is in the same direction as the transverse thrust. Occasionally ships are fitted with inwards turning propellers because this is said to give better speed and steering; but manoeuvrability is poor.

Two engines—one propeller

If a ship has two engines, but a single propeller, the pilot should be told whether both engines are in use all the time, or if one is used for ahead movements and one for astern, or if only one engine is available for both ahead and astern movements. To a pilot, the significance of this system is that he may only have half power available and there may be delays with the clutch when changing from ahead to astern.

Bow thrusters

More and more ships are being fitted with bow thrusters and sometimes with stern thrusters as well. The purpose of these is to give sideways propulsion. They are very useful, provided their limitations are appreciated.

Ship owners tend to fit underpowered thrusters and expect them to do the work of a powerful tug. Thrusters are not of very much use when the ship has a light draught, because they are too near the surface of the water and may even be partly out of the water. Most thrusters lose effectiveness as the ship increases speed and are little or no help at speeds of more than 3 or 4 knots. They may still exert some force until a speed of between 5 and 10 knots has been reached, but the rudder would then be far more effective for turning the ship.

Many thrusters are equivalent to 10–15 tonnes bollard pull which is less than the power of a strong tug; therefore a swinging operation will be much slower than is possible with tug assistance. In a strong wind a ship may make too much leeway in a small swinging area if the manoeuvre takes a long time. If a thruster is insufficiently powerful to dispense with a tug, it should simply be treated as an additional aid.

Although slow to move a ship, thrusters provide a helpful cushion when landing alongside, especially if the wharf is of solid construction. They are also useful when a ship has to berth in a very tight corner with little manoeuvring space for a tug.

Thrusters can be used to assist steering at very slow speed, or to keep a ship's position in the channel without any head-way. This capability is put to good use when the ship is unable to proceed to the berth immediately because of an unexpected obstruction in the channel or a delay in tug availability etc. If a ship should break away from her moorings, a thruster may make the difference between disaster and deliverance from danger.

When navigating stern first, a bow thruster is more useful than a tug, provided the ship is not allowed to gather too much sternway.

Control of the thruster(s) should be according to the pilot's orders. Some thrusters have a variable control from zero to maximum and some have two or three available speeds. There is a tendency on the part of some masters to give more or less power according to their own assessment, in the same way that "adjustments" are made to the main engine control by fiddling with a controllable pitch propeller lever. This tendency may even go so far as to switch the thruster on or off without reference to the pilot. Officers are again advised not to get into this bad habit. A pilot must feel confident that the master and officers are executing his orders as he requires them; he must be able to assume at any time that the ship's behaviour is under the influence of his last orders. A dangerous situation may arise if the pilot calls for full thrust, only to be told that full thrust is already being applied—the pilot thought he still had something up his sleeve but it has gone. When tugs are employed they are always under the control of the pilot (the master may not even understand the tug orders if a foreign language is used); when thrusters are used, they also should be under the control of the pilot.

There are many modern passenger ships and container ships fitted with controllable pitch propellers and thrusters, that a pilot could handle like a dream if he received the assistance to which he is entitled; but he is often distracted because he has to watch not only the ship and the wharf, but the captain as well. If the master thinks more or less power is required from either the main engines or thrusters he should either say so to the pilot, or say nothing, but he should not make changes without consulting the pilot.

THE RUDDER

Research is being carried out into the design and effectiveness of rudders, propellers, and ships' hulls. Much of this work is done on models in simulated conditions. It is important to the pilot and to ships' personnel that research and improvements should be made; some ships are more manoeuvrable than others as a result. However, it is not the purpose of this book to report on these developments; they are best studied as they become available, usually in papers prepared by the researchers.

A pilot must treat all ships with equal respect and preparedness at the commencement of the pilotage. It soon becomes apparent to him how a ship will behave, but he must always be alert for the unexpected happening. The latest designs in rudder and propeller may assist a ship to run more efficiently and economically at sea and may please or disappoint a pilot with their effectiveness, but he is not usually given information about the shape and size of rudder or of the theory or calculations that explain its superior characteristics.

A pilot's helm orders will be the same, whatever rudder the ship possesses; but he will find that he needs less angle of rudder on some ships than on others for the same result.

Many years ago, a maritime law was introduced which insists that helm orders to right or starboard are only to be given if it is intended that the ship's head shall move to the right or starboard; left or port helm orders are to move the ship's head to the left or port. The reason for this law was the confusion that could arise if the steering gear was so designed that the rudder moved in the opposite direction from that in which the helm was turned. For example, in a small boat, the tiller is moved to starboard in order to turn the rudder and the boat to port; this was once normal practice in larger vessels.

Earlier Collision Regulations had a rule which stated "... right rudder or starboard to mean 'put the vessel's rudder to starboard'; etc...." The latest International Collision Regulations contain no such rule, but this should always be the intention.

In actual practice, a pilot does not always intend the ship's head to go in the direction of a helm order (but he always intends the rudder to go that way). If a ship is swinging quickly the pilot may order opposite helm to slow the swing but with no intention of reversing it. When the ship's head continues to swing against the helm, the master or officer may become unnecessarily alarmed that the ship is not answering the helm or does not have enough steerage way. The master may be tempted to suggest more engine power or even to give a burst on the bow thruster. However, it is almost certain that the pilot is fully aware of the situation and is judging the swing and assessing the need for his next order.

Some of the helm orders given early in the pilotage will be for the purpose of gauging a ship's responsiveness. A pilot may order an experimental 10 degrees of rudder approaching a turn, fully expecting to need 20 degrees and allowing plenty of time to apply the additional rudder angle.

A helm order may be given by the pilot in anticipation of a situation that might not arise. For example, in the final approach to the berth he may put the rudder hard over one way or the other so that he can move the stern of the ship sideways by a short burst on the engines. If the anticipated movement is not required, the officer on the bridge will be left wondering at the need for an ineffective helm order.

The rudder can also be used to slow down the ship, by turning the wheel from hard over one way to hard over the other way with engines stopped.

The maximum rudder angle available (hard over) is usually 35 degrees each way. At some time or other this angle was chosen as the minimum requirement and was thought to be close to the optimum. Some vessels have been fitted with rudders capable of wider angles of operation, with good results.

If the ship is moving forward with engines turning, speed is reduced when rudder is applied. This is noticeable when negotiating sharp turns in pilotage waters. The reduction in speed is partly due to drag on the rudder and partly due to the skidding motion of a ship when turning. If the rudder is held hard over so that the ship completes a full circle, the speed may be reduced by as much as 50%, even if the same revolutions are maintained throughout the turn. Very often the revolutions are seen to fall when the ship is turning under a large angle of rudder.

Effective steering cannot be expected when a ship has sternway. It may be attempted and the result will vary from one ship to another and depending upon wind and other influences on the ship's movement. It is most likely to be successful with several knots sternway and engines stopped.

In short pilotages and during the manoeuvre into or out of a berth, the work of the man at the wheel is not very demanding, mentally; it may be physically demanding if the ship has a large heavy wheel. He performs an important part in ship-handling, but not on his own initiative. His duty is to do exactly what he is told. The pilot should make the helmsman's work as straightforward and uncomplicated as possible by giving clear, concise orders. Helm orders should give a number of degrees to port (or left) or to starboard (or right). The number of degrees ordered indicate the rudder angle that is required. The rudder indicator should be clearly displayed so that the man at the wheel and everyone else on the bridge can check it at a glance.

The number of degrees of rudder has nothing to do with the number of degrees in the ship's compass heading. If the order is, say, "starboard ten" the rudder must be turned to an angle of starboard ten degrees—and it must be kept there until the next order is given. The man at the wheel should repeat the order and should report when the order has been executed. Helmsmen sometimes turn the wheel the wrong way, or fail to keep the rudder at the angle that was ordered.

Master, officers and pilot must all be alert for such errors. Pilots would prefer the retention of large, conventional ships' wheels, because it is possible to see out of the corner of one's eye whether the helmsman is applying wheel in the required direction. Ships are fitted with a variety of steering innovations such as miniature wheels or tillers, joy-sticks and push buttons; these may be quicker and easier for the man at the wheel but they are more prone to error and often it is not possible to see from a distance how the "wheel" is being applied.

On some ships the engine room telegraph is alongside the wheel and the helmsman operates both wheel and telegraph—he may even have to answer the telephone as well. This is not a good idea, he should be allowed to concentrate on the wheel only.

Apart from specific degrees of helm, the only other orders should be "hard-a-port", "hard left", "hard-a-starboard", "hard right", "amidships" and "steady". The pilot should steady the ship's head himself with a rudder-angle order followed by "amidships" before ordering "steady"; this ensures that the ship is on the heading that is required. If "steady" is ordered when the ship's head is swinging, there may be some doubt about what course should be steered.

The helmsman may steer a compass course or he may steer by a distant light or object ahead of the ship. It is generally preferable to steer by the compass because distant lights and objects have a habit of going out or moving or becoming obscured. A good helmsman may use both methods simultaneously. Small alterations to the ship's heading may be ordered as a course to steer without giving helm orders.

In the early or later stages of a manoeuvre, the pilot will rarely give the order "steady"; he will prefer to know exactly how much helm is being applied at any time and will confine his orders to angles of rudder.

Helm orders such as "starboard a bit (more)", "ease the helm", "check her", "meet her", "port easy" etc. are too indecisive for good ship-handling and should not be used. Another commonly used, but ill-advised helm order is "nothing to port (or starboard or left or right)". The inference is that there is an approaching danger on the side indicated in the order. If a course is to be steered properly there should be "nothing" to port and "nothing" to starboard, except for a very small permissible wandering which depends upon the skill and concentration of the helmsman and other relevant factors such as speed, trim, wind, sea etc. If the helmsman is directed not to, allow the ship's head to wander at all to port, then the actual mean course he steers becomes something to starboard of that which he has been given. A more sensible action on the part of the navigator is to alter course a few degrees away from the danger. Avoiding the danger is the responsibility of the person in charge; the man at the wheel has only to do what he is told and he should not be given confusing orders or unnecessary responsibility. Limiting the number of phrases used also reduces the chances of misunderstanding when there is a language problem.

When approaching a very sharp turn with little room to spare, it is desirable to put the wheel first amidships to see if there is any turning moment influencing the ship apart from action of the rudder; this also allows availability of full rudder either way. The ship's head is then started in the required direction towards the turn. It is important to start a turn in plenty of time, but slowly. It is much easier to speed up a slow turn by applying more helm, more engine power or tug assistance, than it is to check a swing in the wrong direction and get the ship moving the other way. The time taken to reverse a swing, if not properly judged, may take the ship aground or so far ahead that the turn cannot be completed without going astern on the engines. Some engines cannot be speedily changed from ahead to astern and the pilot has an agonising decision to make when it looks as though the ship may not make it round the corner.

When turning out of a channel or across a channel, it is important to look astern, in case there is harbour traffic overtaking. There may be local laws about certain vessels keeping clear of others, but in addition to this the International Collision Regulation apply—and so do the rules of good seamanship.

SHIP BEHAVIOUR

Practical ship-handling does not require the memorising of formulae and hypotheses that are the result of extensive calculation and experimentation. Many of these results are incomplete and inconclusive. Calculations, simulations and experimentations have been going on for hundreds of years and will continue.

What is necessary, is to have a basic knowledge of what may be expected to happen and why it happens. It is also very important to be prepared for the unexpected.

The transverse thrust of the propeller has already been mentioned. This is probably the most important predictable behaviourial characteristic of a ship. However, a ship does not always "cut" the way she is expected to. When sternway is gathered, the cut may continue or the ship may move in a straight line or even sidle her stern the other way.

If a ship is stopped by putting engines full astern when the ship is making full speed ahead, there is no predicting what path she will follow or what the heading will be when way is lost. Full astern is not necessarily the quickest way of taking way off a ship. Speed automatically drops when engines are stopped from going ahead, because of friction on the sides of the ship, but a propeller turning very fast astern does not grip the water immediately. It is just as effective to go slow astern and gradually build up astern revolutions as the ship's headway drops. This problem should not arise when man-oeuvring in a harbour, because headway will always be kept under control.

Transverse thrust is accentuated when the ship is in shallow water, which is usually the case when approaching a

34

berth. However, an astern movement close to a solid wharf face thrusts water between ship and wharf and tends to move the stern away from the wharf. Conversely, an ahead movement sucks water from between ship and wharf; this causes a pressure drop and the ship is drawn towards the wharf. An ahead movement alongside the wharf is usually accompanied by a helm order in a single screw ship.

Wind, current, draught, trim and proximity to the bottom, all influence a ship's behaviour. The bottom of a harbour is seldom flat; it has deeps and ridges, mud, rock, shifting sand, weed and debris. These variations cannot be simulated, but they cause irregularities to currents, eddies and pressure differences.

Squat

As a ship moves through the water, she squats, i.e. sinks closer to the bottom than when she is at rest. Higher speed and less depth of water increase the squat. This must be taken into account when allowing a safe under keel clearance in restricted channels. This closeness to the bottom also affects steering, which will be more sluggish than in deeper water.

Banks

Just as a ship is attracted by the proximity of the ground under her keel, so she is attracted towards ground on either side. When a ship passes close to the side of the channel or close to a bank or shallow patch, the escape route of the displaced water is restricted; the water moves faster on the restricted side, a pressure drop occurs and the ship moves towards the side of lowest pressure, i.e. towards the bank. In practice it is the stern that moves most noticeably towards the bank and the bow moves away. The forward rotation of the propeller also draws the ship and the bank together. The wedge of water between the ship's bow and the bank, pushes the bow away. This attraction and repulsion is an important consideration when negotiating bends in a channel or river; it is used to advantage when turning at the outer side of the curve but opposes the turn if the ship gets close to the point. If

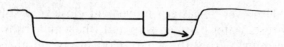

Fig. 10—*Ship attracted to nearest bank.*

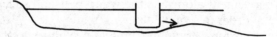

Fig. 11—*Attracted to shallow patch.*

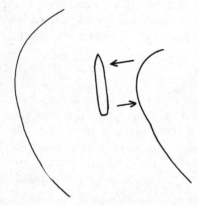

Fig. 12—*Bow repelled, stern attracted.*

a point is approached too closely, the bow will be deflected towards the opposite bank; the stern will then be attracted by the point and it may be impossible to keep the ship in the channel. Of course there are other considerations to be taken into account when navigating a channel, such as depth of water and flow of the current; it must not be assumed that it is always wrong to approach the "point side" when making a turn.

Another situation in which this attraction occurs is when passing close to another ship.

Meeting head on

If the channel is wide enough to allow each ship to pass the other without deviating from its course there should be no problem. If both ships require to be close to the centre of a narrow channel, the passing is not so straightforward and a good understanding is necessary between the pilots on the two ships. Neither ship should alter course too soon, because this would place it at a dangerous angle across the channel. Each ship should alter course to starboard at the same time when quite close to each other end on. The bows of the ships will repel each other and this will have to be countered by opposite helm to bring the ships parallel. The sterns will attract each other and this also has to be countered by use of the rudder to bring the ships back to the centre of the channel.

Overtaking

This is more dangerous than meeting end on. Unless the overtaken ship is almost stopped, the time taken can be quite considerable. Suppose a large ship is overtaking a smaller ship. The larger ship will exert the most influence. First, the bow will repel the other ship as the overtaking commences; this will cause the bow of the smaller ship to swing towards the path of the larger ship. When the bows come level, the

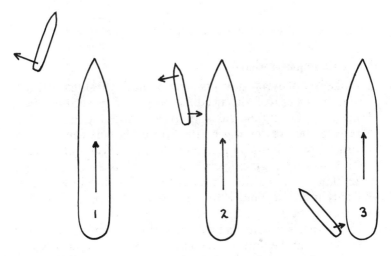

Fig. 13—*Smaller vessel in difficulty when overtaken.*

smaller ship will be forced the other way, and this movement will then be increased by the attraction of the two sterns; by this time the smaller ship may be out of control and could be drawn into a collision before the two are passed and clear. See Fig. 13 positions 1, 2, and 3.

Passing a ship at anchor

This requires extreme care, because the ship at anchor is not able to take any evasive action and there is a serious risk that the unsecured stern of the anchored ship will be sucked towards the passing ship. If a close quarters passing is unavoidable it must be remembered that the interaction between the two ships will be minimised by reducing speed and by stopping the engines.

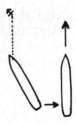

Fig. 14—*Vessel at anchor attracted by passing vessel.*

Passing a ship at a wharf

This is an every day occurrence and all ships' officers should be aware of the need to keep a ship securely held alongside. The closer the ship passes and the faster it is travelling, the greater will be the attraction between the two. A turning propeller also increases the attraction, but it is not possible to stop engines every time a ship passes another. It is quite likely that the sudden movement of a ship in her berth will part mooring lines if they are slack; the possible consequences can be easily imagined.

A passing ship can get into a very discomfiting position where little can be done to keep away from the other. Engines must be stopped to reduce both speed and propeller attraction. The bow will have a natural inclination to move away. If the stern comes in dangerously close to the other ship, engines must be started again and speed gradually increased with rudder hard over towards the moored ship.

Even more care is required when a ship passes close to another in order to enter an adjacent berth. The moving ship has to make allowance in her approach for attraction; but if the moored ship has neglected to keep lines tight she will come out to meet the other. If lines part there will be a good chance of a collision.

Three important rules should avoid accidents in the foregoing circumstances: Pass other ships slowly. Do not pass too close. Keep a ship properly moored in her berth.

Fig. 15—*Lines parting as ship passes.*

Wind and current influences

A ship under way with neither wind nor current to affect her progress meets practically negligible air resistance. Power is required only to push through the water. When the air moves and becomes a strong wind, it can have a very important influence on the ship and it may assist or hinder ship-handling. A current opposing the wind creates the problem of balancing one against the other.

A pilot has knowledge of the current to be expected during a manoeuvre and is aware of likely variations due to certain circumstances. Harbour currents are not entirely predictable by reference to charts and tide tables. A neap tide sometimes produces a strong current. Irregular currents are caused by storm water and factory discharges. Recent heavy rain causes a "freshet" which increases the flow of water in a river port.

The direction of a current is indicated by small craft lying at anchor—not by large craft because these take more time to swing at the turn of the tide and may be lying into the wind irrespective of the current.

An appreciation of surface current may be gained by observing the water that is passing ends of wharves and buoys and by the movement of floating debris. It must be remembered when these observations are made at close range, that water is being disturbed by the propellers of ship and tugs and by the ship's motion.

Continuous appraisal of wind direction and force are necessary during a manoeuvre. Changes occur with little warning. Anemometers are not always part of a ship's equipment. The pilot does not spend all his time in the wheelhouse—if he did, he might not be aware of the wind; he must go to each wing of the bridge from time to time to keep fully in touch with the situation. It is always helpful to have a flag flying above the bridge for a quick check on the relative wind; it is worth leaving a flag up at night-time for this purpose.

A deeply laden ship may not be greatly affected by wind; but high sided ships such as passenger ships, container ships, liquid gas carriers, car carriers and empty bulk carriers or tankers, may be very difficult to control in an unfavourable wind. Current usually has a greater influence than wind when a ship is at a deep draught unless the wind is extremely strong.

A ship that is stopped in the water and allowed to drift will take up a position with the wind on the beam. Thus it can be seen that there is a tendency to turn the ship broadside to the wind when the ship is stopped or moving ahead slowly. When a ship has sternway, the stern seeks the wind until way is lost.

If a ship is decelerated when there is a current at an acute angle to the ship's course, the ship will have the same inclination to turn abeam to the current that she has in a wind. Once way is lost relative to the water, she will drift at the whim of the current and may change direction if the current varies.

Current is not always the same strength or even flowing in the same direction deep in the water as it is on the surface. In a river or tidal channel, the current is stronger in the middle than at the sides and is (usually) stronger at the outer side of a curve than close to the point. There may be a counter current near the point. A ship may get into an awkward situation if she unintentionally or unavoidably has one extremity in water that is moving fast and her other end in still water. This difference in current is used to advantage when swinging a ship.

Pivot point

This is a point in the ship's axis about which she turns or pivots. Its position and its mobility play an important part in ship-handling. For example it will be seen that the *centre* of a swinging basin is not always the ideal place to commence swinging, because one end of the ship may need more swinging room than the other.

Fig. 16—*Swinging with pivot point well aft.*

The pivot point is not (necessarily) amidships. Its position depends upon the shape of the hull and the centre of pressure on the hull and other factors.

A ship which is identically shaped at each end will have its pivot point amidships when at rest. A more usual initial position is forward of amidships. However, it is not a fixed point; it moves forward or back depending upon forces acting on the ship.

Trimming a ship by the stern moves the pivot point further aft and trimming by the head moves it forward. Sternway causes the pivot point to move aft, but under headway it may be only a quarter of a ship's length from the bow. This is an important fact to remember when attempting to swing away from danger. In shallow water the pivot point does not move as far forward as it does in deep water.

D

When a ship is swung by applying a force at one end only, the pivot point will usually be closer to the other end of the ship; whether the force is by rudder and propeller or from a tug. If the force is applied closer to amidships, the pivot point will move further away. The position can be reached where the ship will pivot about one end. This must be considered when placing tugs.

HARBOUR AIDS

Channel marks

Ships' officers will be aware of the buoyage system in use in a particular port and will be able to recognise a port hand buoy from a starboard hand buoy etc. However, this is not sufficient information to be able to navigate safely and in accordance with local practice.

The master of a ship becomes understandably concerned if his ship is taken close to a concrete knuckle or a rocky point that he can see clearly above the water; but he may be content to almost touch a starboard hand buoy on his starboard side. Some rocky points are in very deep water, but a channel marking buoy does not always mark the edge of a channel. The nature of the bottom may not allow a buoy to be placed in the ideal position, or it may be deliberately placed in shallow water to widen the channel for the benefit of shallow draught shipping; this allows the lighter ships to keep clear of larger, deep vessels that need the centre of the channel. The pilot knows how far he must be from the buoys to maintain sufficient depth for the ship he is piloting. In some cases it is perfectly safe to pass on the "wrong" side. Not all of this can be explained to the master while the ship is being manoeuvred, it must be taken on trust.

"Leading marks" or "Ranges" are not always what they seem to be. They are not necessarily two marks or lights which must be kept in line ahead or astern. They may be for the purpose of separating traffic, or they may indicate the edge of a shoal or the side of a channel. They may be temporary leads used by a dredger, with no navigational significance to anyone else. They can be confusing to the master of a ship

43

entering a strange port. The officer on the bridge should observe all navigational marks and endeavour to interpret their significance by reference to the chart.

Speed of approach indicators

The purpose of these is to indicate to the pilot the speed at which each end of the ship is closing the wharf. The information may be shown from the wharf as a visual display of coloured light signals or a dial giving the actual speed, or it may be transmitted to an instrument on the bridge. Pilots become proficient at judging whether a ship is coming alongside too fast, but in the case of very large heavy ships, the momentum is so great that landing must be extremely gentle and the speed indicator serves to reassure (or warn) the pilot and the master.

Some ports also have equipment that indicates to the pilot his position in relation to the centre of the channel and his forward speed over the ground.

Radio communication

VHF is a boon to the pilot. He can give orders directly and precisely to tugs, he can communicate with other ships, receive information about shipping movements; he can check information about berth availability and delays and he can summon assistance or give instant reports in an emergency. In some ports he is given valuable information to assist him with pilotage in poor visibility. Communications and traffic systems are more advanced in some ports than others, but radio is essential to ensure smooth running efficiency in a busy port.

Radio discipline is important. Messages should be brief and should be expressed in standard radio phraseology. Excessive chattering can saturate a radio channel and interfere with important messages. A manoeuvre may be jeopardised if a critical signal is lost between pilot and tug.

During a berthing operation it is helpful if the pilot can communicate by radio with the mooring launches and with the person who is in charge of the wharf.

Bridge mark

This is a simple device but a very helpful one to the ship-handler. It usually comprises a board, about one metre long with the word "Bridge" clearly printed on it. At night a small light is required to illuminate the notice. If the pilot can see exactly where the bridge of the ship is required, he will conduct his manoeuvre accordingly, otherwise he may come alongside 100 metres or 2 metres out of position and there will be much shouting between wharf and bridge to indicate where the ship should be berthed.

Coming alongside exactly in the place allocated to the ship allows lines to be run correctly, but if the ship is out of position it takes a long time to move just a short distance. If necessary, information should be sent in advance by the pilot giving the ship's overall length and the distance from bow to bridge.

Wharf construction

Depending upon its type of construction, a wharf may be either an aid or a hazard to ship-handling. A hard, un-protected wharf face poses problems. Even in large ships there may be only three or four men on deck at each end and there is no one available to lower fenders between ship and wharf.

Very old wharves also need to be approached with great care. Wharves which were adequate for sailing ships and small steamers are not always suitable for large heavy ships. Port development is expensive and slow. The master of a ship may be excused for thinking that he is only being put at an old wharf in the hope that his ship will knock it down and his company be forced to pay for the repairs.

The pilot must always do his best to come alongside gently and without damage to ship or wharf. Sometimes he is so gentle that he would not break an egg and yet the old wharf creaks and growls as if it were about to collapse.

Modern fendering makes a very important contribution to successful ship-handling. Fendering may be a complex mech-anical or hydraulic system that allows movement of the wharf face, or it may be a series of rubber fenders secured along the full length of the wharf. If rubber fenders are large enough they make very satisfactory cushions against a solid wharf and they also provide an efficient brake to check the ship's fore and aft movement.

Corners of wharves, or knuckles as they are called, are often neglected. They may be fendered at a later date—after a few ships have been scratched or dented, and it has been shown that fendering really was necessary.

It must not be thought that a pilot can approach a well fendered wharf with gay abandon and expect the rubber padding to absorb or cancel any deficiencies in his judgment. A ship must always be treated as a fragile article. The hull of a ship is sometimes called the "shell"; it should be treated as an egg shell, not as an oyster shell.

Wharves can be damaged quite easily, no matter how well they are protected. Many ships have fine lines forward and aft; they have flared bows and cut away sterns; even ugly ships may have yacht-like contours at water level or wharf level. A bad approach can cause the flare of the bow or the stern to ride over the top of the fendering and strike the hard edge of the wharf.

Wooden pile wharves are more susceptible to damage than solid wharves; particularly old wooden piles which have been worn away to a fraction of their original thickness. Floating fenders, suspended fenders and projections from the hull are potential pile snappers, because they bring all the weight of the ship to bear on one point.

Bollards

At the completion of a berthing operation, the ship must be well secured to the wharf. A good, well designed wharf will have numerous bollards and they will extend well beyond the berthing limits of the ship. If necessary they will be situated inshore from the face of the wharf to provide safe storm moorings in the event of strong winds. A well designed ship will have many points from which mooring lines can be run and will be well equipped with lines, winches and fairleads.

Experience has shown that neither ships nor wharves are always equipped as they should be. A lot of money is spent later, installing additional bollards on wharves and additional fairleads on ships. A ship is sometimes expected to tie up in a berth that is shorter than the ship itself; this presents problems because fairleads and mooring winches are situated at the ends of the ship and are designed to lead beyond the ship at each end.

Mooring problems are also encountered with ships that have very high freeboard, such as liquid gas carriers and some container ships.

Ships' officers in charge of mooring parties must be sure not to put all their lines on one bollard. It is quite conceivable that a bollard could be wrenched from its foundations if it is given too many lines; on an old wharf this is even more likely to happen. The men handling the lines on the wharf or in mooring launches do not always know the best place to which lines should be run and it is the responsibility of the officers to ensure that sufficient lines are used and that the load is spread as evenly as possible. The pilot will help in this matter according to normal practice at the berth and with regard to the exposure of the berth to winds, current and passing ships. A pilot never leaves a ship until she is safely moored in the berth.

USE OF ANCHORS

Single anchor

When there is plenty of room for anchoring, the operation is fairly straightforward. Anchoring in a confined space or on a particular spot is not so easy and must not be treated lightly.

Anchoring provides a good opportunity to observe a ship's behaviour.

There are two recognised ways of approaching an anchorage. The first is to take off all headway before letting go. This is a good procedure when anchoring in very deep water when it may be necessary to walk out three or four shackles of cable before the anchor reaches the bottom. The anchor should not be dropped from the pipe in such deep water because the windlass brake may not be able to stop so much weight of cable from running out and the entire cable with anchor attached could be lost.

Anchoring without headway is satisfactory when the exact anchorage position is not critical. The engines can be used astern to stop the ship, and the anchor dropped as the ship starts to gather sternway. Slight sternway is maintained while the cable is run out and it may be necessary to go ahead on the engines to stop the ship again when sufficient cable has been run out. If possible this manoeuvre should be carried out with head into the wind or stemming the current, so that the ship finishes up in the position in which she is expected to lie; otherwise it is necessary to wait while the ship swings to wind or current before it can be seen that the ship is safely anchored with sufficient cable. When the ship has settled down to her anchorage, is not dragging the anchor and has a steady strain on the cable, she is said to be "brought up".

When anchoring within harbour limits it is usual to be

confined to a specific anchorage location. This is because of limited space depending upon the ship's draught or to allow the maximum number of ships to use the space available. This is often a cause of concern to masters because the shore looks very close when viewed from the bridge at an inside anchorage; other ships also look very close. Sometimes there appears to be a better and larger anchorage elsewhere, but that one may be reserved for a larger ship.

In order to drop the anchor accurately it is necessary to maintain control of the ship until the moment of letting go. Only if the ship is fitted with a bow thruster, or if tugs are in attendance is it satisfactory to anchor by the method previously described. Otherwise when engines are put astern it is usual for the transverse thrust of the propeller to cause the ship to sheer off course. No action of the rudder is likely to stop this sideways movement; although it may be anticipated to some extent by giving the ship a swing in the other direction before going astern, there is no guarantee that the swing will be reversed by an astern engine movement.

Apart from the transverse movement caused by going astern on the engines, the ship may be set or blown out of position by tide or wind. It is not always possible to choose the best direction from which to approach.

To keep control of the ship, steerage way is required and it is best to let go the anchor when moving ahead. An astern engine movement may be given briefly in the approaches to check that the engines *will go* astern. Speed should be judged so that all way can easily be taken off after the anchor has been dropped.

The pilot will know the correct position for the bridge of the ship at the moment for letting go. This will depend upon the ship's heading and the distance from bridge to forecastle, with a few seconds allowed for releasing the anchor. Provided the anchor is dropped on the right spot it does not matter which way the ship is heading at the time. The ship will swing and settle down to the most comfortable position she can find and the time she takes to do this is of secondary importance when precision anchoring is required.

The officer on the forecastle plays an important part in anchoring. There are two vital rules of procedure that he must follow. First, he must let go the anchor the moment he is given the order. Second, he must not allow the brake to be applied too soon.

Windlass equipment must be checked beforehand. If there is any doubt about the anchor falling from the pipe it should be walked out prior to arrival and held on the brake just clear of the water. On some ships it is usual to walk out the anchor to avoid damage to the bulbous bow.

Care must be taken not to let go before the order is given. This is even more serious than letting go late, especially if the ship has considerable headway. Much depends upon good communications between bridge and forecastle to ensure that orders are understood.

If there is a delay after the order has been given before the anchor is dropped, the ship may pass out of the allocated anchorage and it will be necessary to make another approach. Apart from the inconvenience to the ship, this may disrupt other harbour movements.

When the anchor cable is running out, there is concern among forecastle personnel that the anchor is getting away and must be stopped. It *must not* be stopped too soon. It will naturally run out fast because it is very heavy and this is accentuated by the ship's headway. A full shackle or more of cable may leave the ship before the anchor hits the bottom. If the brake is applied too soon after letting go while the ship has headway or sternway, the anchor will be dragged along the bottom and the whole manoeuvre will have to be done again to place the ship once more in the right position. When two or three shackles have run out it should be possible to apply some brake pressure and then to release cable gradually as the ship loses way.

The officer should report each joining shackle to the bridge, but he may miss the first two and should not prematurely stop the cable simply to check the number of shackles. When the required number has run out, the brake should be applied firmly and the ship allowed to settle down.

However, the brake should not be applied too hard if the ship still has headway. A small ship or a light ship can be pulled up by a tight cable, but a heavy deep laden ship may snap the cable or burn out the brake. Although the anchor cable can support a steady strain, even against the ship's engines, it cannot be expected to hold against a sudden jerk. It is better to release more cable and to pick it up when the ship finally stops.

The amount of cable used will depend upon depth of water, draught of the ship, wind, current, nature of the bottom and the time that the ship is expected to remain at anchor. Within harbour limits, three to five shackles of cable would be usual. There may be occasions when more is required, but on the other hand there may not be sufficient swinging room to use any more.

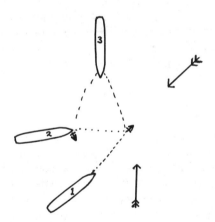

Fig. 17—*Dropping second (starboard) anchor as wind veers.*

There is no firm rule that can be used as a guide to which anchor should be used; but there are preferences that apply in certain circumstances. If an anchor is likely to be used in a berthing operation after leaving the anchorage, it would be usual to use the same anchor, because there is a reasonable assurance that *that* anchor will do what it is told, the second time. One anchor may not be available. It is a tidier operation to use the windward anchor when letting go under headway. The possibility of having to drop a second anchor later should also be taken into account; for example: if a ship is to lie to a North Easterly wind and there is a likelihood of the wind veering to South and strengthening, it would be better to have the port anchor down first so that the starboard anchor can be dropped when the change comes and one cable will not foul the other. See Fig. 17. This choice would depend upon knowledge of local conditions.

The officer on watch should plot the ship's position on the chart and should make a note of the bearings in the log book. This should be normal practice even if the ship is only anchored for a little while; the time spent at anchor sometimes extends much longer than expected. The position should be checked frequently. If the ship appears to be dragging her anchor, this can be verified by reference to the original position and bearings. It may be necessary to pay out more cable and/or drop the other anchor. It may also be necessary to call for a pilot at once to move the ship to another position.

Heaving up the anchor

If there is a strong wind or current, the strain on the windlass can be eased by steaming ahead towards the anchor. If the anchor has been dropped in unexpectedly deep water, it may be necessary to heave in as much cable as possible and then steam into shallower water to enable the windlass to lift the anchor off the bottom. This is an unlikely occurrence within harbour limits unless the windlass is in very poor condition. Many windlasses are in poor condition.

Leaving the anchorage

Departing from an anchorage provides another useful opportunity to observe the ship's manoeuvring characteristics; especially if it is necessary to turn round before proceeding with the pilotage.

Turning circle

There may be sufficient room to turn the ship by going ahead with the rudder hard over. Some knowledge of the ship's turning circle is required. A number of factors determine the size of turning circles. The transverse thrust of the propeller when going ahead tends to assist a turn to port, and consequently, the turning circle to port is normally smaller than to starboard. Increasing speed does not necessarily reduce the size of a turning circle—in fact a turn at slow speed is usually tighter than a turn at full speed. Draught and trim also make a difference. A light ship will turn in less space than she would need when fully laden and trimming by the stern further reduces the turning circle. When listed, a ship turns more easily to the low side. More space is required to turn in shallow water.

The safest procedure is to give a strong burst on the engines to commence the swing and then slow down so that way can be taken off without too much trouble in the event of the ship requiring a wider circle than was expected. The rudder should be kept hard over.

If the ship is likely to make too much leeway before she can be safely turned round, it is advisable to steam around the anchor and to heave up when facing the desired direction. It would be usual to shorten up the cable to one or two shackles while making this turn.

Turning short round

By the use of engines and rudder, a ship can be turned round in little more than her own length. In a single screw ship the first movement should be astern with rudder amidships. It is always a relief to see that the engines will go astern. Should the engines fail, the ship can be anchored again immediately. By going astern first it will soon be seen whether the ship "cuts" with the screw. The stern will probably turn into the wind as sternway is gathered, irrespective of any transverse thrust from the propeller.

The initial turn of the ship indicates which way she wants

to go, and it is generally advisable to turn in that direction rather than to attempt to force the ship around against her own inclination. Before much sternway has been gathered, the engines should be put ahead with the rudder hard over in the direction of turn.

Whether full ahead will be required or whether slow ahead or less will be sufficient will depend upon the power of the ship. In a modern powerful ship, full ahead and full astern are only used for urgent necessity, and even half speed is seldom called for; but in a small or underpowered ship, full ahead and full astern may be required to get sufficient response. The first ahead movement with rudder hard over will accelerate the swing and by the time the ship starts to gain headway, the engines should be moving astern again. This procedure is repeated until it is certain that the ship can be turned onto the desired heading without further astern movements.

A twin screw ship can be turned round by applying one engine ahead and the other astern. As with a single screw ship, the turn will be easier if the stern is swung into the wind. If space does not demand that the ship be turned in her own length by exactly balancing one engine against the other, the turn may be speeded up by allowing alternate headway and sternway—this enables more effective use of the rudder.

Two anchors

A ship lying to a single anchor requires swinging room with a radius equal to the length of the ship plus the length of cable that is being used. If there is not sufficient room for this,

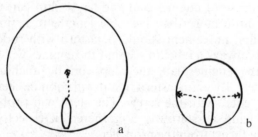

Fig. 18—(a) *Swinging room required at single anchor.* (b) *Swinging room with two anchors down.*

it is necessary to use two anchors to restrict the ship's movement; see Fig. 18.

Running moor

The purpose of this exercise is to drop two anchors with the cable of each in line with the other and the bow of the ship approximately midway between the two anchors. The direction in which the cables are laid will be either to allow maximum safe distance from dangers on each side, or to provide the best holding for the anchors in the two chosen opposite directions. In the case of a tidal channel or river anchorage both of these reasons may apply; see Fig. 19.

The first anchor is dropped in a predetermined position while the ship is steaming ahead, as would be done for a single anchor. The ship is kept on a steady course. Speed is gradually reduced so that the ship can be brought to a stop when the position is reached at which the second anchor should be dropped. The amount of cable used on the first anchor must be equal to the total length of cable that will be out on both anchors when the manoeuvre has been completed.

The ship should have slight sternway when the second anchor is dropped, to ensure that the cable does not pile up on top of the anchor and foul the flukes. The ship should be given a sheer to swing the stern away from the cables as the first one is hove in and the second is paid out. The ship will be finally moored with equal cable on each anchor, or slightly more on one if it is known that the wind or current will be stronger from one direction than from the other.

When departing from a running moor, one cable must be slacked away while heaving on the other. The last anchor to

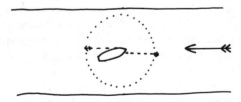

Fig. 19—*Two anchors used in a tidal channel with limited swinging room.*

be picked up would normally be the one in the direction in which the ship will be proceeding when leaving the anchorage. If this is not an important consideration, the last anchor should be the one to which the ship is riding at the time of commencing to heave up.

There are disadvantages with this mooring arrangement. The amount of cable used with each anchor can only be approximately half the length of cable that is fitted on either side. If, for example, there are nine shackles of cable on one anchor and seven on the other, the anchor with the longer cable would be dropped first and the ship could be moored with just over four shackles on each. If there were only seven shackles on each anchor, this would be insufficient in some circumstances for a running moor.

If a strong wind blows across the line of the cables, a tremendous strain is put on them and neither is correctly positioned to take the strain.

It is quite likely that the ship will unavoidably have turns in the cables at the time she has to leave the anchorage. One cable can be unshackled and the turns taken out by laborious seamanship, but the only satisfactory and quick ship-handling method of removing the turns is to employ a tug to push the ship round until the turns have gone—being careful to push in the right direction! It is usually futile to try to steam round and take the turns out that way.

Standing moor

This is an alternative procedure to the running moor, but the end result is the same. The first anchor is dropped with the ship stopped in the water, or just gathering sternway, and the cable is paid out while the ship comes astern to the position in which the second anchor is to be dropped. The ship may come astern under her engines or may fall back from the influence of wind or current. Cables are then equalised.

Open moor

Two anchors are used, but the cables are laid in such a way that one anchor is on each bow; see Fig. 20.

Fig. 20—*Open moor.*

The manoeuvre is carried out as follows. The first anchor is dropped while the ship is moving ahead. The ship is turned gradually to port if the port anchor has been dropped first, so that the cable is laid in a curve. The starboard anchor is dropped when the port cable is almost at the bitter end—depending upon the amount of cable available. Before dropping the second anchor, all headway must be off the ship and she must be just commencing to come astern so that the anchor will dig in and the cable will not foul the flukes. While slacking away on the starboard (second) cable the port cable is hove in, as is done with a running moor, and the ship is manoeuvred astern into a position at the apex of a triangle formed by the two cables; see Fig. 21.

A ship at anchor is held by the weight of cable, not just by the flukes of the anchor. A large ship has very heavy cable and it is not possible to pull the cables into perfectly straight lines when backing the ship to its final position at an open moor.

A ship moored in this way is not intended to swing round as she would at a single anchor or at a running moor. Both anchors share the strain most of the time.

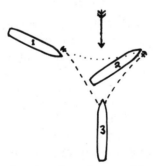

Fig. 21—*Dropping first (port) anchor, position (1); dropping second anchor, position (2); backed into final position (3) for open moor.*

If the anchors and cables are laid too far apart they will be weaker than a single cable—this can be seen as a simple triangle of forces. The ship is held against wind or current over an arc from one anchor to the other with a minimum of swing. Should the wind become so strong that the ship drags her anchors, they will tend to draw together right ahead and the ship will then have the best possible security from two anchors with equal cable on each and more cable available if required.

An open moor is used if the wind or current is sure to be from the same direction, or at least from the same quarter, for the duration of the ship's stay at the anchorage. It is also used in conjunction with mooring buoys in some tanker ports and sometimes with stern moorings to the shore; see Fig. 22.

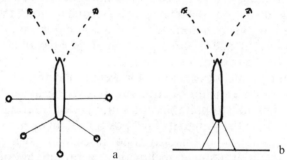

Fig. 22—(a) *Moored to anchors and buoys.* (b) *Moored to anchors and shore lines.*

The approach to this mooring and also the choice of which anchor to let go first will depend upon the manoeuvring room available and the conditions of wind and current at the time.

If the approach must be made from the opposite direction to that in which the ship will be finally moored, it is desirable to drop the starboard anchor first, so that the engines going astern can be used to assist with turning the ship.

When there is more room to manoeuvre and the approach can be made at little more than 90 degrees to the final berthing direction, either anchor may be used first. If there is a strong wind or tide helping to line up the ship in her berth, there will be no need for assistance from transverse thrust of the propeller and a port anchor first manoeuvre will be preferable. As the ship comes astern to equalise the cables, an astern movement of the engines will help stop the ship from swinging too quickly.

Securing to buoys takes quite a long time and the ship must be held in position after anchoring while lines are set up. Except in perfectly ideal conditions, a large ship will need tugs to assist and it may also be necessary to await favourable conditions. Such berths are usually sited head to seaward and berthing is done on a flood tide.

Anchor to assist berthing alongside

An anchor is sometimes used in the approach to a berth, either as part of a prearranged plan or as an emergency measure.

When used according to plan, an anchor steadies the ship's head and slows her progress so that she may be steered with the engines going ahead, but without gaining too much headway. The bow of the ship can be brought close to the wharf, using the anchor to prevent a heavy impact even with an onshore wind, and the rest of the ship is then swung around the anchor into position alongside. When headway has been taken off, it may be found that the anchor has a strong grip on the bottom; a few links of cable are then slacked away to allow the ship to come gently alongside forward and the ship may then be pivoted about this point.

There are advantages in using the lee anchor when

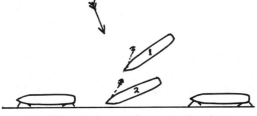

Fig. 23—*Anchor used to assist berthing.*

berthing a ship that is flying light and making leeway towards the wharf. The ship passes over the anchor, and the cable leads under the ship's hull and holds the ship bodily against the wind instead of only holding the bow. The anchor grips the bottom more firmly because the cable is leading from the ship's bilge and not almost vertically from the hawse pipe. The friction between cable and ship's side eases the strain on the windlass. When using the engines ahead, with lee rudder to hold the stern up into the wind, better leverage will be applied if the anchor cable is leading down the lee side of the ship—going ahead on engines against a weather anchor tends to swing the stern further to leeward.

The inside anchor must not be used if the ship is close to the bottom. When a ship passes over its own anchor there is always a risk that the anchor could puncture the hull if there is very little keel clearance.

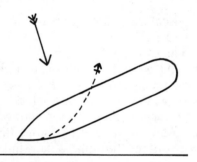

Fig. 24—*Using lee anchor.*

The amount of cable used when approaching a wharf would usually be between one and two shackles, depending upon depth, draught and nature of bottom; it may only be necessary to have the anchor just on the bottom. The officer on the forecastle head must put the brake on *early* because it is intended that the anchor shall be dragged. When an anchor hits the bottom, the cable becomes slack momentarily; this is the time to apply the brake—not hard, but firmly enough to control the cable. If too much cable is run out before applying the brake, the ship will be pulled up too soon or the cable will snap. It may be necessary to delay dropping the anchor until late in the approach to the berth to avoid deep water or telegraph cables; or it may be a late decision by the pilot. The officer forward and the person operating the windlass must be ready to let go an anchor at any time. A ship-handler has to rely on forecastle personnel; the need for care and efficiency when handling anchors cannot be over-emphasised.

The emergency use of anchors occurs when a ship approaches its berth too fast. This may be due to an engine delay or other reasons. An anchor will be used for the express purpose of slowing the ship's progress. Possibly both anchors will be dropped together. The officer forward will be told to "hold on" soon after dropping; but he will have to take care. If the brake is applied too soon, or not at all, the anchors will not reduce the ship's speed. If the brake is applied too late or too suddenly it may burn out the brake linings or snap the cable.

When there is a danger of the ship ramming a wharf or going aground, it is usual to drop anchors. It has been said since time immemorial that "you must never go aground with anchors in the pipe". This was good advice in olden days because the offshore anchors could be used later to heave the ship afloat. It is still good advice in some circumstances. However, there are times when an accident becomes so inevitable and imminent that dropping an anchor will do no good whatsoever. Unfortunately, the pilot and master will be criticised and possibly condemned by those who sit in judgment if an anchor is not dropped in accordance with time honoured custom.

Anchor used as an additional mooring

At some wharves it is desirable to use the anchor as a supplementary mooring. It may be a port authority rule that ships are berthed head to seaward with an anchor ahead of the ship.

The anchor is sometimes dropped in the approach to the berth so that it can be used to heave the ship off on departure. It may also be used as a holding off mooring at an exposed berth to prevent damage to ship or wharf caused by movement of the ship while lying alongside. In the latter case, the anchor only holds off the forward end of the ship and adequate fenders or holding off moorings may be required aft.

Whatever the purpose for using anchors, the officer on the forecastle should be well briefed beforehand. He should ask for this briefing. He should also be prepared for unscheduled use of anchors at any time.

Dredging

A ship may be controlled, to some extent, by use of anchor and rudder. In order to change the ship's position at anchor, the cable is shortened up until there is only sufficient to check the ship's head but not to prevent dragging. The ship is given a sheer by turning the rudder towards the direction in which it is desired to move and the ship is allowed to drag the anchor under influence of the current. When a satisfactory new position has been reached, the cable is slacked away so that the ship rides to her anchor again.

Phraseology

Other terms are sometimes used for the anchoring and mooring work described here. Nautical jargon is changing; many older expressions are falling into disuse and to perpetuate any of these would be an affectation. For example, when an anchor is used with a minimum of cable it is more usual to order that the anchor be dropped "on the bottom" instead of the more nautical "at short stay". In fact, the term "at short stay" has at least three different meanings in connection with anchoring. A good reason for not using archaic expressions is that their original meaning is not known or understood; it is better to avoid them than to try and define them. Terms which have a geographical origin are not in common usage any more.

Fathoms are being replaced by metres, but in this book the term "shackle of cable" (also known as a "shot" in some quarters) has been retained and refers to a length of fifteen fathoms.

MOORING LINES

Lines are used not only to keep a ship safely in her berth, but also to assist with ship-handling.

First, there must be a clear way of identifying the lines. When securing to buoys, the lines take the names or numbers of the buoys. Alongside a wharf the following terminology should be used:

Lines leading at right angles to the ship's heading are called *breast lines*; in the fore part of the ship they are forward breast lines and at or near the stern they are aft breast lines.

Lines that lead at an acute angle forward from the fore part of the ship are called *head lines*.

Lines that lead at an acute angle aft from the stern are called *stern lines*.

Lines leading aft from the fore part of the ship or forward from the after part of the ship are called respectively *forward springs* and *aft springs*.

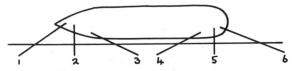

Fig. 25—*Mooring lines:* (1) *head line,* (2) *forward breast line,* (3) *forward spring,* (4) *aft spring,* (5) *aft breast line,* (6) *stern line.*

No other names are required. Terms such as forward back spring and after fore spring are sometimes used but are superfluous and confusing.

The basic names given here are the ones in most common usage and are in accordance with the standard marine vocabulary recommended by IMCO. See Fig. 25.

At various times in their careers all ships' officers will be in charge of the mooring crew at each end of a ship. When reporting to the bridge before going to stations, officers will be given instructions; but there are some things which an officer should know without being told every time.

When a line is run to the shore, this should be done as expeditiously as possible. As soon as the eye is on the wharf bollard, surplus slack should be heaved inboard. Once a ship is alongside, the lines should be heaved tight as quickly as possible. It is frustrating to the pilot to bring a ship neatly alongside, only to see it drift off again because the officers and crew are too slow with their lines. On the other hand, it is not correct to heave away so fast that one end of the ship is brought suddenly into the wharf while the other end flies off. Each officer can only bring one end alongside, but he must be sensible and watch the whole ship as well as he can. There is no prize for being first into the wharf.

A spring should be sent ashore as soon as possible. This will be used to check the ship's movement along the wharf. Care must be taken to slack away when too much weight comes on the line, otherwise the ship will be brought too rapidly into the wharf, or the line will part and its usefulness lost. To "check" does not mean "hold on, come what may!" The same caution is required when the ship is moving ahead against a stern line or moving astern with a tight head line: see Fig. 26.

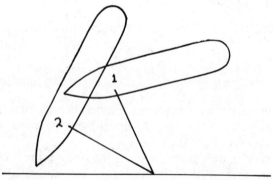

Fig. 26—*Bow pulled into wharf by a tight line.*

Once the ship is alongside and in position, at least one line must be made fast at each end immediately to hold the ship in position. This must be done before running bights of lines or additional lines or shifting lines to other bollards. The first lines to be secured can be shifted later if necessary, but it is important that the ship be held firmly as soon as she has arrived, otherwise she will drift off and there will be a tangle of lines hanging uselessly.

Undermanning is a problem when tying up and letting go. Patience is required. An attempt has been made to make up for reduced manning by fitting mooring lines to large winch drums. These stay on the winch, there is no need to use a stopper or to turn them up on bitts. On many ships these winch lines are inadequate on their own and it is necessary to use additional moorings. It takes a long time to secure a ship, or to single up for departure, when there are only three or four men at each end.

"Singling up" is the procedure of letting go most of the lines a few minutes before departure time so that the final letting go can be done quickly. A common instruction is "single up to one and one"; this means take in all lines except a spring and one other line at each end, i.e. a total of four lines to be left out ("one and one" at each end). When singling up in a strong offshore wind, care must be taken that the ship does not break away from the wharf when some of the lines have been taken in. It is not always possible to handle more than one or two lines at each end simultaneously and it may be necessary for a tug to hold the ship alongside while she is singled up.

At some berths shore moorings are used. These are often in the form of large rope snotters which are used by passing a ship's line through one eye and back on board. The other eye of the snotter is put on a wharf bollard. These are used when there is a surge at the berth, or likely to be very rough conditions.

SINGLE BUOY MOORING

The most natural way to approach a buoy is to head into the wind or current. A stationary ship is very quickly blown or set out of position and it is necessary to overcompensate for this when making an approach with a cross wind or current. However, there is not always sufficient room to allow much choice and the direction of approach is not of paramount importance if tug assistance is available.

A ship must be brought to the buoy slowly so that it can be stopped with a minimum use of astern engine movements. If speed is too fast, and it is necessary to go full astern or half astern, the transverse thrust may throw the bow away from the buoy and it will not be easy to bring the ship back into the correct position; any advantage hoped for by heading into the wind will be immediately lost as the bow is blown further away.

The anchors must be well and truly secure. They should not be dropped in close proximity to a buoy under any circumstances, as they may foul the buoy's moorings or, more disastrously, rupture submarine pipelines. This eventuality can be avoided by making a slow approach to the buoy and using tugs if necessary to hold the ship steady at the buoy. If there is plenty of sea room all around the problem does not arise.

Using buoy equipment

The manoeuvre should be fairly straightforward when using lines that are permanently attached to the buoy. Single buoy moorings at oil terminals have heavy duty synthetic rope, and chain, with a long light-weight line for heaving the other on board. The inner end of the mooring is secured to the ship by a slip or a shackle or a large snotter or strop. This inboard equipment may have to be passed to the ship on each occasion from an attendant launch and may also be accompanied by a person from ashore to assist with the mooring operation. The line which is first hove on board is sufficiently long to enable the end to be picked up when the ship is still well away from the buoy. It is not necessary for the ship to come too close to the buoy and she should not be allowed to do so.

An oil terminal buoy has floating pipelines for connection to the ship. The ship's initial approach to the buoy should be on the side away from these floating pipelines. If the buoy is situated in a confined space, it may be necessary to use tugs to hold the ship off while the moorings are secured and until she has settled down to her riding position.

Some buoys are situated in the open sea and are designed to support a ship in quite rough conditions, but buoys in shallow water can only be used when the conditions are more favourable.

Using ship's equipment

There may be occasions when a ship secures to a buoy with her own mooring lines. This is a simple operation but is not a satisfactory all-weather arrangement. It is practically impossible to equalise the strain on several lines to a single buoy, and they may all part one by one if the wind suddenly freshens.

The most secure way for a ship to lie at a buoy is with the anchor cable shackled on. This necessitates a much more precise manoeuvre by the ship-handler. The cable of a large ship is very heavy and cannot be manhandled. The ship must be brought into such a position that the end of the cable is immediately above the ring on the buoy.

The anchor must first be hung off and the cable disconnected. This is more easily said than done. If joining shackles are not regularly taken apart, unshackling takes a long time. A word of advice to the officer in charge on the forecastle: be sure that the anchor is hung off *securely*. The inboard end of the short length of cable attached to the anchor must also be secure.

It is usual to lead the cable out through the hawse pipe to the buoy. Sometimes a fairlead on the deck is used if the cable can be handled.

When approaching the buoy, a good line must be run from the after end of the forecastle on each side. These are secured to the buoy and the ship is then hove up close by these two lines until the buoy is alongside the ship and directly underneath the free end of the anchor cable. These lines must not be run from right forward because that would not allow the ship to be positioned correctly—they would be vertical before the buoy could be brought under the cable. See Fig. 27.

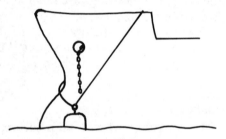

Fig. 27—*Heaving ship into position for shackling cable to a buoy.*

A head wind or current assists to slow the ship when nearing the buoy, and also assists with the steering; but it is not always possible to choose such an approach. Provided the first two lines are run quickly, the direction of approach is not important. Shackling a buoy to the anchor cable is not a quick or easy job and the ship must be held in position by the two first lines throughout the remainder of the operation, irrespective of wind, current and weather conditions. The ship will pivot about the buoy and find her own most comfortable direction of repose.

The time taken to shackle on depends upon sea conditions at the time and on the type of construction of the buoy. Some buoys are very difficult working platforms under any conditions. One or two tugs may be required to assist with positioning and to ease the strain on the ship's lines.

When the cable has been secured to the buoy, *all other* lines should be let go, so there is nothing to foul the buoy, cable or shackle. When departing from the buoy it may be necessary to use a line to hold the buoy steady while the cable is unshackled. A slip line is most suitable for this purpose, i.e. a line passed from the ship through the buoy ring and back on board. This slip line should not be run until shortly before departure.

The amount of cable out to a buoy should be enough to form a slight catenary. If a very strong wind comes up, it may be advisable to veer out more cable to ease the strain.

USE OF TUGS

To be a successful ship-handler it is necessary to make the best possible use of whatever tugs are available. To do this, a pilot must be familiar with the capabilities and limitations of his tugs and tug masters. This knowledge cannot be gained by reading the tugs' specifications, nor can it be fully understood by observation from the bridge of a ship. Tug masters are experts in their own specialised field and pilots should accompany them on tugs from time to time to improve appreciation of each other's problems. This should be done on every type of tug that is used in the port. Ships' officers should do the same thing if they can find the time; it will help in their training.

Developments in tug design and propulsion have been just as dramatic as changes in other areas in the shipping industry. However, tugs have to be strong and durable and they are only used at their maximum capacity for comparatively few hours in a working day, therefore they have a long life. Consequently, there may be a wide range of tugs in use in any one port, from the oldest most unmanageable tug to the very latest in power and manoeuvrability. Pilots must know the relative merits and shortcomings of all tugs in the port.

There are some Cinderella ports which have to make do with hand-me-down tugs that have not been worn out but are not wanted elsewhere. Pilots and tug masters in these ports are often blithely unaware of how handicapped they are by not having the benefits of modern tug technology.

To the layman it appears as if the tugs are doing all the work when a ship is being handled. To the ship-owner, tugs are an expense that should be avoided or minimised as far as possible; the master of the ship may also see them in this light. The observant officer will see that the tugs are not acting on their own initiative, but in response to a carefully devised plan and to specific instructions from the pilot.

There are times when a ship could be handled with one or two tugs less than the number used. In some cases a tug is used when it is not absolutely necessary. As with insurance, it is better to have it and not need it than to need it and not to have it. There is usually a good reason for the number of tugs that is used; it is not simply a matter of estimating how many tugs are needed at that time.

Ships are costly to operate and they cannot be kept waiting indefinitely—nor can they be allowed to delay others—in the hope that more favourable conditions may allow the manoeuvre to be carried out more cheaply.

The use of tugs protects ships and other property and helps to keep the port operating efficiently. For some manoeuvres, tugs are virtually essential and to attempt to handle the ship without tug assistance would be foolhardy.

A pilot does not see tugs as instruments for making his job easier, nor does he see them merely as emergency aids in case he cannot manage without. Tugs are integral parts in the performance of ship-handling.

Types of tugs

(i) *Single screw, single rudder.*

This was once the description of practically every harbour tug. Powerful engines in a small hull, one large propeller and one large rudder. Steam or diesel engined and very manoeuvrable compared with an average cargo ship. There are still many tugs in service that answer this basic description, but they are very unmanoeuvrable compared with tugs of more advanced design.

(ii) *Twin screws with one, two or multiple rudders.*

It has already been stated that twin screws are an advantage in a powerful ship. Tugs have more power for their size than cargo ships and manoeuvrability is much improved by fitting twin screws.

(iii) *Fixed nozzles.*

The bollard pull of a tug can be increased considerably by channelling the propeller thrust through a fore and aft cylinder, or nozzle as it is called. Directional control is also improved because a rudder at the outer (aft) end of a nozzle is more effective than the rudder behind an open propeller.

(iv) *Steering nozzles.*

With this system, the propeller operates in the usual way, but the nozzle turns and directs the thrust at an angle up to 40 or 50 degrees to the fore and aft line, allowing the tug to be steered and turned with less power loss than is the case with conventional rudder steering.

(v) *Omnidirectional propulsion.*

The foregoing developments have been accompanied by increased power for assisting with the handling of very large ships. However, fixed nozzles and steering nozzles used with fixed propellers are, at best, only slight improvements on conventional twin screw propulsion. All of these tugs are designed for operating with engines going ahead and they can usually manage little better than 50% of ahead bollard pull when pulling astern.

More advanced systems have been in use for many years. Tugs which can move in any direction with equal facility are fitted either with "cycloidal" propulsion or with "rudder-propellers" that can be rotated through 360 degrees. The two systems are quite different and there are a number of variations. All these omnidirectional tugs will be referred to in this text as "tractor" tugs. Their capabilities and versatility are very similar and that is what matters to the ship-handler. Horse power (or its metric equivalent), means nothing. A pilot needs to know what type of tug he is using and what is the bollard pull ahead and astern. Two tugs may have the same horse power but vastly different bollard pull. If a pilot knows he has a tractor tug with 30 tonnes bollard pull ahead and 29 tonnes astern it does not matter to him if the horse power is 2000 or 3000.

In a port which handles all shapes and sizes of vessels in a variety of situations, tug versatility is essential. It is important to have tugs that can push or pull with (almost) the same power whether going ahead or astern. Tractor tugs can also move sideways and can spin round in their own length; "Conventional" tugs pale by comparison and it is a wonder that tug operators continue to build and use anything but the best—presumably the reason is associated with cost.

Securing the tug

(i) *On the hook.*

The towing hook of a conventional tug is situated amidships. The reason for this is to allow the tug to move her stern either way by use of rudder and propeller and so change direction by pivoting about the towing hook. If the hook were at the stern, directly above the rudder, the tug would be held helplessly by the towline as soon as weight was applied.

An amidships towing hook has its dangers. If the tug gets in such a position that it is heading at right angles to the towline, there is a possibility that the tug could be capsized by its own line. A tug caught in this situation is said to be "girded". Rolling right over may be averted at the last minute by operating a quick release mechanism on the hook or by breaking the line; but these alternatives are also to be avoided if possible. Tug masters are always alert to the danger of girding; but the ship-handler also has a responsibility for the safety of the tug. A pilot knows his tugs and knows which are most vulnerable to this particular danger. A tug must be given sufficient time and room to get into position and to change position. It is sometimes necessary to handle a ship to suit the tug. An unsuitable tug or a poorly handled tug can be more of a liability than an assistance.

Another potentially dangerous situation arises when a tug

Fig. 28—*Tug girded.*

F

is taking a head line from the ship. The tug should not approach too close to the bow of a ship that has headway; there is a danger that the tug could be run over. It is safer for the tug to take up position abeam of the ship's forecastle within heaving line distance. The line can be passed to the tug and once the line is on the hook the tug will move away until the towline is the correct length for the manoeuvre.

Tractor tugs are able to operate on a towline without fear of girding. Depending upon the type of tractor and the maker's preference, the propulsion is either aft in the usual place or it may be about one third of the tug's length from the bow. In either case the towline may be used from the end of the tug. If the propulsion is aft, the towline can be right forward; if the propulsion is forward, the towline would be right aft. Even if the tug's engines break down it cannot be capsized by girding (see Fig. 29) because the tug will be pulled around into the direction of the line. Manoeuvrability is good because the towing hook is well away from the propulsion.

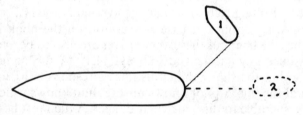

Fig. 29—*Towing hook aft avoids girding.*

A towline tug is useful when lifting off from a berth, swinging, or for steadying the ship's head in a narrow channel. A conventional tug is very limited in the assistance it can give while on a towline; it can only pull, and it cannot quickly change the direction of the pull. A more manoeuvrable tug can change position more readily, but is still restricted.

(ii) *Alongside*

The alternative to a towline is to secure the tug alongside the ship. This is done by lines from the fore part of the tug (or from aft if that is more convenient). Any tug secured in this way is well placed for pushing. By going astern it can also pull, but its pulling capability is limited unless it is a tug with equal astern and ahead power. A single screw tug has practically no directional control while pulling from this position. By visualising a simple parallelogram of forces it will be seen that the resultant pull is further reduced when the tug's line comes from a lead on the ship that is much higher than the tug. Some ships are fitted with suitable securing points set into the ship's side at a convenient height for a tug's line. Unfortunately, many ships are built without sufficient thought being given to the need for securing tugs.

The best tug alongside is a tractor with propulsion aft. No tug works efficiently sideways when lashed up fore and aft alongside, because of the strain on the lines at each end. It is necessary for the tug to direct its pushing and pulling at one point. When a tug is pulling a ship from this position, water from the propulsion units is forced against the ship's side and this tends to move the ship in the opposite direction to that which is intended. Therefore it is advantageous to have the tug's propulsion as far away from the ship as possible.

(iii) *The best position*

This depends upon the nature of the manoeuvre. It also depends upon the disposition of bitts, the ship's draught and the adaptability of the tug. It is not always possible for the pilot to use a tug in the position he would prefer; sometimes the tug master must insist on an alternative for his own safety. There is also the possibility of the tug pushing a hole through the side of the ship; on some ships the tugs are only allowed to push at certain designated places.

If a manoeuvre is to be carried out in a swell it is not possible to have a tug alongside. Movement in the swell might damage either the ship or the tug as the two collide, and the short lines would most likely carry away.

(iv) *Suction pads.*

Some tugs are fitted with an articulated contraption forward with a large suction pad at the outer end. The tug fastens to the ship like a limpet and can push or pull as required. This system is very effective for moving large, high-

sided ships and it saves time and man-power because there are
no lines to be handled. However, it cannot be used on all ships
nor in all situations.

(v) *Ideal tug.*

The ideal harbour tug for ship-handling assistance has
equal power ahead and astern; it can move in any direction
and can change position from one side of the ship to the other
without putting unwanted weight on the towline. Instead of a
towing hook it has a large winch drum at the bow or the stern
(at the opposite end to that at which the propulsion units are
situated). A line is permanently attached to this winch drum
and can be used as a towline or for holding the tug alongside a
ship. Using a control in the wheel-house, the tug master can
shorten or lengthen this line in a few seconds.

(vi) *Other factors.*

Determining the manner in which a tug shall be secured,
often becomes a matter of local preference, depending upon
the type of tugs in the port, the situation of the berths, the
wind and the tide. Local practice sometimes becomes a matter
of habit and, to an outsider, it may appear as though the tugs
are not always used to best advantage.

There is also the question of whether to use the tug's line
or the ship's line. The ideal tug has a line of known breaking
strain that can be retrieved very quickly. With an old
fashioned single screw tug it is more convenient to use a ship's
line on the hook because it can be easily released and left to
the ship's crew to recover; this is particularly convenient if the
tug is required for further assistance; e.g. it may have to let go
the towline and then make fast alongside.

If the ship does not give a good line to the tug, the ship-
handler is handicapped. When a towline parts during a
manoeuvre, the tug master invariably condemns it as a poor
line, and the ship's officer usually reports it as having been the
best line in the ship—if not brand new. The pilot's comments
may be unprintable.

The number of men in the tug's crew, also their skill,
willingness and self-imposed work limitations are also factors
to be known and taken into account. It may not be possible or

permissible to handle a line that enables use of a tug's full capabilities.

Number of tugs required

There are many ports that have no tugs at all, and some ship-handlers have never used a tug. In certain circumstances tugs are unnecessary, but to study practical ship-handling without studying the use of tugs is barely scratching the surface of the subject.

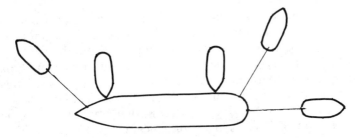

Fig. 30—*Tug power in all directions.*

It is quite common to use three or four tugs or even more on a large ship. If the tugs are sufficiently powerful and versatile, four should be enough for any manoeuvre (provided the ship's engines are also available). Four tugs enable the ship to be pushed or pulled either way at each end. If more than four tugs are used, the reason will be that the tugs are considered to be underpowered or of an unsuitable type for the particular ship or for the conditions at the time; or it may be because the ship itself is underpowered and additional tugs may be required to supplement the main engines. See Fig. 30.

The pilot must be the one who ultimately decides how many tugs should be used. He is the one who will be doing the job, and only he can know and assess the numerous factors that must be considered. The master of the ship is entitled to request a minimum number of tugs but he should not attempt to talk the pilot into reducing the number. The harbour master may also insist on a minimum number, for the safety of the port.

It is usual to have a regular method of determining the number of tugs to be used, so that everyone concerned can make arrangements in advance. It is not practicable to treat each job on its merits at the last minute. There is usually a scale from "no tugs" to the maximum number, based on the tonnage and/or length of ships. Some ships are individually categorised because of special features. A powerful bow or stern thruster may be accepted in lieu of a tug. The nature of the manoeuvre is also a factor, e.g. if the ship has to be swung or navigated stern first.

Economic considerations and industrial relations also have bearings on the number of tugs used. It cannot be expected that there should be an unlimited number of tugs available at any time of the day or night; this would be unreasonable to request of tug owners or tug crews. Tugs must be ordered in sufficient time to be available when required. For a Sunday afternoon they may have to be ordered on Friday. This sometimes leads to the use of additional tugs to cover the possibility of unfavourable weather conditions.

The total number of tugs in a port must be a compromise. Volume of shipping has its peaks and troughs. If there were sufficient tugs in a port to attend every ship when traffic movements are at a peak, most of the tugs would be idle most of the time. As all tugs have to pay their way, this would necessitate higher charges; so it is better to tolerate minor delays from time to time.

Even the smallest ships may require tug assistance. Whereas a large ship may use four or more tugs, it is unlikely that a small ship would ever need more than one or two. A port that caters for ships of all sizes should also have tugs of all sizes from 5 tonnes bollard pull to 50 tonnes or more.

It is not always possible to allocate the most suitable tugs to a particular ship. At a port where tugs vary in type and power, it may be necessary to order additional tugs to cover the eventuality of the superior tugs not being available. Two of the best tugs may be a better combination than three or four of the others.

A visiting ship master and his officers do not always appreciate all the problems that are involved. They might be excused at times for thinking that their ship is operating for the benefit of people other than their owners. A fairer way of putting it may be to say that those who provide the service are just as important as those for whom the service is provided. A successful port or shipping industry depends upon co-operation of all who are involved—and so does successful ship-handling.

Communications

If there is no radio, the pilot must call the tugs alongside the bridge and pass his preliminary instructions the best way he can. During the manoeuvre, orders to push or pull etc. are usually given by mutually agreed hand whistle signals. This method is reasonably effective when handling a small ship, but it is far from satisfactory on a large ship with several tugs in attendance. It is also very difficult for a tug master to hear whistle signals over the sound of his noisy diesel engine— especially if he is inside the air-conditioned wheel house of a modern tug.

VHF radio is not used in all ports, but it should be treated as a necessity, not a luxury. Most tugs and ships are fitted and very often the pilot carries his own set with him. A pilot usually carries a hand whistle too, in case the radio breaks down.

Communication procedures between pilot and tugs vary from one port to another. All radio messages should be clear and concise. It may be necessary for the pilot to give preliminary instructions to the tug masters, and an outline of his intended manoeuvre. After that, his orders should be brief.

In some ports it is the practice to number the tugs on each ship and to call them by number. It is more usual for the pilot to prefix his orders with the name of the tug. The important thing is to have a system whereby there can be no doubt about which tug is being called. There may be several ships operating on the same frequency and such terms as "forward tug" and "after tug" are not positively identifiable.

Most orders to tugs can be restricted to "ahead", "astern" and "stop"; when a tug is on a towline the tug master must also be told in which direction to pull.

A tug master may anticipate a pilot's next order and be in the right position at the right time; but he should never push or pull until he has been given the order to do so. This is for the same reason that the ship's main engines and thrusters must not be varied without the pilot's instructions. The pilot must be in overall charge of the situation all the time, and must know what power is being applied and what power is still available.

An understanding between pilot and tug master is essential for good ship-handling. Too much weight on a tug's line at the wrong time, or not enough, can wreck a manoeuvre. On the other hand, a skilful tug master has averted an accident on many occasions by good anticipation and quick response.

The pilot knows the power and capability of each tug. When a tug is told to go ahead or astern, the amount of power that is applied will depend upon the understanding between pilot and tug master; this is part of the pilot's local knowledge. In some ports the pilot tells the tug master exactly how much power he requires, just as he does with the ship's propulsion. It is more usual to leave the initial response to the tug master's discretion and for the pilot to call for more or less power as required. When a tug is working alongside a moving ship, a proportion of its power is used to keep the tug in position at an angle to the ship's side.

Communication between pilot and tug master is not confined to orders and acknowledgments. A tug master is able to give advice regarding distance off and closing speeds. This is useful supplementary information to that received from the ship's officers. In some circumstances however, when working alongside a large ship, the tug master can see nothing of the manoeuvre, or of the ship except that part to which the tug is secured.

TO AND FROM THE WHARF

Berthing

There are basically three ways of approaching a berth: head in, stern in, or swinging off the berth. For the purpose of the following examples it will be assumed that a single screw ship has a right handed propeller and a twin screw ship has outward turning propellers.

Head in

Head in, port side to, is generally considered to be the most straightforward of all berthing operations. The berth is approached at an angle as shown in Fig. 31.

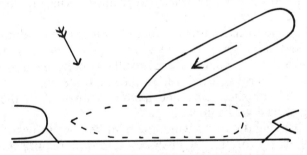

Fig. 31—*Head in port side to.*

Speed of approach is judged so that an astern movement will easily stop the ship before the bow strikes the wharf, and so that the transverse thrust of the propeller will bring the stern towards the wharf.

If the angle of approach is too fine, the transverse thrust may swing the stern too quickly into the wharf. The same thing can happen if speed of approach is too fast—more astern revolutions will be required and the stern will cut into the wharf before headway has been stopped.

If the angle of approach is too wide and the speed too slow, the astern movement required to stop the ship will not be sufficient to swing the stern alongside. The manoeuvre will be an untidy one, with the fore part of the ship alongside and the after part well off. Ahead movements with rudder hard-a-starboard followed by astern movements will be necessary to turn the ship into position. When there is an offshore wind or a following current, it may not be possible to get the ship alongside from this situation; it may be better to abort the manoeuvre, back out and try again with a smaller angle of approach. If the wind is onshore, the ship will eventually come alongside without further engine movements.

Head in, starboard side to, requires a finer angle of approach, because the astern movement will throw the stern away from the wharf. Slower speed is called for when berthing starboard side to, so that the ship can be stopped with a minimum of stern power. If possible, before going astern, the bow should be given a sheer away from the wharf to counter the expected transverse thrust.

When performing this manoeuvre without tugs alongside it is essential to get lines ashore at each end as soon as possible so that the ship does not drift out of position. A pilot should only have to berth the ship once, but sloppy work by ship's crew or shore-side line handlers can lead to the job having to be done again.

If there is little or no wind, the pilot will head towards the middle of the berth. An offshore wind will require an approach towards the nearer end of the berth whereas an onshore wind may necessitate an approach that is directed further along the wharf, to allow for leeway as in Fig. 31.

Bank suction must be allowed for if there is shallow water near the edge of the channel in the approaches to the berth.

An anchor may be used to help with this manoeuvre, as explained on pp. 59/60.

Depending upon the size of the ship, one or more tugs may be used to assist berthing. If only one tug is used, it will almost invariably be placed forward and probably secured alongside. A ship, like a horse, has the main propulsion aft, but in each case the handler must control the head.

Exact positioning of the tug will depend upon the contours of the ship. A flaring bow may necessitate taking the tug as much as one third of a ship's length from the stem; this is not necessarily a disadvantage if the tug's effectiveness in that position is understood.

A tug that is secured right forward when pushing or pulling the bow will cause almost equal and opposite movement of the stern (when the ship is stationary). A tug that is placed one third of a ship's length from the bow will exert much less influence on the ship's stern, will cause less turning moment but more bodily movement sideways.

Fig. 32—*Tug alongside, pulling like an anchor or pushing.*

The main purpose of the forward tug is to allow a gentle landing on the wharf, by holding off prior to impact. In the approaches to the berth, the tug acts as an anchor by coming astern when required to check the ship's speed; it can do this effectively while being dragged along by the ship without any need to angle out from the ship's side. The tug is more useful than an anchor because it can pull or push, or do neither. In the event of an offshore wind, the tug is required to push up to the berth and prevent the bow from being blown away.

The placing of a second tug involves a number of options, mainly depending upon the type of tug and the direction and force of wind or current; see Fig. 33.

Tug No. 1 in Fig. 33 is in the position that allows most versatility; it can push or pull to either side or directly in the fore and aft line. Being right aft, it can idle along without causing any drag on either side of the ship when it is not

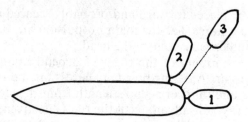

Fig. 33—*Three positions for a tug aft.*

required to push or pull. However, this position is only suitable for a versatile tug and definitely not for a single screw tug.

Tug No. 2 cannot exert the same leverage as No. 1, but it is in the position that must be adopted if the ship's draught or the shape of the stern does not permit securing right aft.

Berthing a ship with two tugs alongside is quite different from berthing without tugs. Port side to is preferred when no tugs are used, because the transverse thrust is used to assist; but the reverse is true when two tugs are in attendance. The transverse thrust is used to help prevent the stern from coming in too fast.

A wide approach must be made when berthing port side to with tugs. This avoids bringing the stern close to the wharf too soon. The after tug may not be able to hold the ship against the cut of the propeller and the stern could come in fast. A wide approach makes allowance for this and, however wide the angle may be, the after tug can compensate by pushing.

When a ship has headway, a single screw tug secured on the starboard side is not as effective as one on the port side.

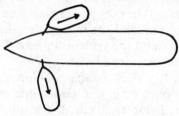

Fig. 34—*Single screw tugs pulling astern, to starboard and to port.*

When the tug pulls astern on the starboard side, its own stern cuts in towards the ship, but on the port side it swings out and gives a more direct pull. This is another point in favour of berthing starboard side to; see Fig. 34.

Tug No. 2 in Fig. 33 causes a drag on the side of the ship, like a large rudder alongside. This must be allowed for in the angle of approach to the berth, whether going starboard side to or port side to.

Before giving the order "astern" to a tug which is on the ship's quarter, the ship-handler must be sure that the resultant pull will be in the appropriate direction. Normally this order would be given with the intention of holding the stern off the wharf. If the tug is unable to open out from the ship's side at a reasonable angle, its resultant pull will have the same effect as going astern on the off-side engine in a twin screw ship; i.e. the tug will pull the stern towards the wharf instead of away from it. This can happen if the ship is moving fast or if the tug is unmanoeuvrable. See Fig. 35.

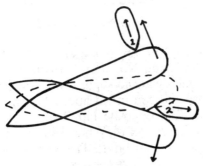

Fig. 35—*Tug alongside aft:* (1) *pulling the stern to starboard and* (2) *stern to port.*

When a tug pushes on the stern or on the quarter (positions 1 and 2 Fig. 33), there is a component of this push that gives the ship headway. This is not a disadvantage, but simply another factor to be kept in mind by the ship-handler. Conversely, when the tug goes astern it has a tendency to reduce the ship's headway.

The after tug may be used on a stern line, as shown by tug

No. 3 in Fig. 33. This is desirable if the tug is unmanoeuvrable or has poor stern power, and if there is a strong onshore wind which can be countered by holding the stern off with a tug on a towline. The same reasoning will apply if there is a strong current across the end of the berth or passing under the wharf.

A tug alongside aft is usually preferable to one on a stern line as there is always the danger of a sternline parting and fouling the propeller.

If a third tug is needed for a head-in berthing, it is usually placed forward. The ship's head must be kept under control at all times, and this can be achieved by having one tug on a head line and one alongside.

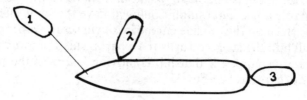

Fig. 36—*Three tugs for berthing.*

Referring to Fig. 36, tug No. 2 alongside forward pushes towards the wharf; tug No. 1 on a towline holds off when necessary, also pulling ahead slightly at the same time. In this way, a very close and controlled approach can be made. The fore part of the ship, opposite No. 2 tug, can be coaxed to within a few centimetres of the wharf before the ship is finally brought alongside at that point. The aft tug then pushes the stern in.

The main disadvantage of a head line tug is that it inadvertently applies weight on the line when this is not wanted. If this is avoided by allowing the line to hang too slack there is a time lag before weight can be applied without jerking the line.

An alternative combination is to use two tugs alongside forward and one aft. This avoids the disadvantages of a head line tug. Sometimes there is insufficient room for a tug to operate on a line. Two tugs alongside together are very effective when maximum tug power is required to assist with a very deep, heavy ship.

A fourth tug may be used either alongside aft or on a stern line; see positions 4 and 5 in Fig. 37.

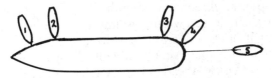

Fig. 37—*Five positions for tugs.*

When placing tugs at or near the stern, it must be remembered that their effectiveness and directional control may be reduced by turbulence from the ship's propeller. At slow speeds this should not be a problem, but full astern in a powerful ship may render a tug impotent.

In a multi-tug manoeuvre it is sometimes helpful to have a tug on a stern line right aft (position No. 5, Fig. 37) for use as a brake. This requires care on the part of the tug master not to part his line. It is useful on a large ship that has poor stern power, or to avoid using the ship's engines astern. The tug may also be used to check the ship's headway while main engines and rudder are applied to cant the stern one way or the other.

Tug placement on a twin screw ship is the same as for single screw, but approach to the wharf can be made at a finer angle because the stern can be controlled by going ahead on one engine and astern on the other. It is possible that twin screws will impose more restrictions on the placement of tugs, depending upon the ship's draught and the shape of the stern.

Approaching a berth stern-first

It is often requested that a ship be berthed stern-in. Many ships must always berth with the same side to the quay because their cargo equipment can only be used on one side. Roll-on roll-off ships are usually built with a stern ramp. It may be a port rule that all ships berth head out, or head to seaward. Sometimes it is more convenient to swing and berth stern-in instead of swinging on departure. It is often necessary to swing a ship and then navigate stern first for some distance before the berth is reached.

There are two distinct disadvantages in a stern-first approach: precise directional stability by engines and rudder alone in a single screw ship is impossible, and the ship is presenting its most vulnerable part to the wharf.

There is also one notable advantage: it is easier to stop sternway by going ahead on the engines than it is to stop headway by going astern.

A twin screw ship may be steered stern-first in good conditions by varying the speeds of the two engines. A ship fitted with twin rudders may be steered by using one engine to give sternway and by applying rudder to the other propeller turning ahead. A dredged anchor can also be used, to steady the ship's head.

To control a single screw ship for any distance stern first along a channel is virtually impossible even in ideal conditions, unless tugs are used to assist.

If only one tug is to be used, the question arises: which end needs the tug most? The answer is—the forward end, because there is already a propeller and a rudder at the stern.

The most effective use of a tug is obtained by placing it right at the stem; see Fig. 38 position No. 1. It can move the ship's bow either way. However, this requires a capable tug, and even a good tug may not be able to work right forward if the ship has an awkwardly shaped bulbous bow.

Position No. 2 in Fig. 38 is satisfactory if the tug is

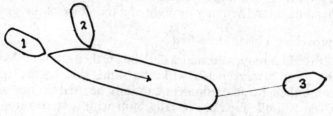

Fig. 38—*Berthing stern first with three tugs.*

powerful and very manoeuvrable; however, it will act as a
bow rudder tending to drag the ship's head to one side, and its
astern-pulling power will be reduced if its lines are secured to
a high forecastle. A tractor tug with an adjustable line is the
most effective in this position; it can keep pace with the ship
by moving sideways, provided the ship does not gather too
much sternway.

A tug that is too unmanageable to be used forward will
have to take a stern line and tow the ship to a position as close
as possible to the berth (position No. 3, Fig. 38). If there is a
wind or current onto the berth it may be necessary to drop an
anchor and then ease the ship alongside by slacking the cable
forward and checking the stern with the towline; see Fig. 39.

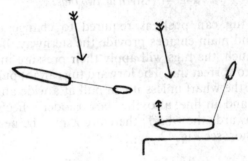

Fig. 39—*Stern in, one tug, wind on the wharf.*

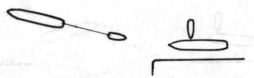

Fig. 40—*Stern in, one tug, no wind.*

If there is no wind or current to assist, it will be necessary
to change the tug during the manoeuvre from a towline to a
pushing up position amidships; see Fig. 40.

The ship should not be treated as if it were dead in this
manoeuvre. The ship's stern can be directed towards or away
from the wharf by going ahead on the engines with the rudder
hard over. The ship must have sufficient sternway to give this

degree of control without stopping the ship's progress until she is off the berth.

When two tugs are employed to assist a stern-in manoeuvre, there is much better control. If the tugs are powerful and manoeuvrable they should both be used alongside; see Fig. 41.

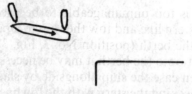

Fig. 41—*Stern in, two tugs.*

Either tug can push as required to change the ship's heading, and main engines provide the sternway. If the stern cuts too much, the tugs will apply their pressure in opposite directions to correct this. The forward tug cannot pull the ship away from the wharf unless it can pull at a wide angle to the ship's fore and aft line; also, the "bow rudder" effect will drag the bow towards the wharf; therefore it may be necessary to use an anchor; see Fig. 42.

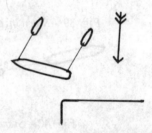

Fig. 42—*Two tugs and an anchor to assist.*

Fig. 43—*Stern in, two tugs, wind on the wharf.*

If there is a strong wind or current setting onto the wharf, or if neither tug is powerful nor manoeuvrable, both tugs will be used on lines. The ship can still be kept under control into her berth, provided the towlines do not part; see Fig. 43.

When three tugs are available, two of them are used

forward to give maximum directional stability; one can push the bow and the other can pull. The third tug is either taken alongside aft, or on a stern line.

Four tugs give complete control with one alongside and one on a line at each end. When four tractor tugs are used it may be more beneficial to have them all on towlines initially and to shorten up the lines on two when the ship nears the berth.

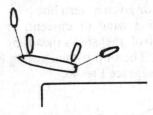

Fig. 44—*Berthing stern in, four tugs.*

Swinging off the berth

It is sometimes necessary or desirable to swing a ship close to the berth. Berthing after the swing may be either head-first or stern-first depending upon tugs and conditions.

With no tugs, wind or current, the ship can be turned short round to starboard and a normal head-in approach can be made. Preferably, the ship would be taken beyond the berth before it is swung, to allow a better approach for berthing. If this is not possible, an anchor can be used and the ship pivoted about the anchor with the bow close to the wharf. A head line and spring must be sent ashore as soon as possible. See Fig. 45.

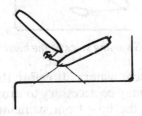

Fig. 45— *Using an anchor to swing off the berth.*

This manoeuvre is also suitable if there is a following wind or current that will help turn the ship.

When there is a strong head wind or current, there should be no attempt to swing off the berth without tugs, because the ship will be set or blown well past the berth by the time the swing is completed. If there is sufficient room, the ship may be taken upstream, swung, and then returned to the berth.

A single tug used to assist the swing can either be secured alongside forward or given a stern line.

With a following wind or current, or none at all, it is preferable to control the ship's head by securing the tug alongside forward. The ship is then swung head to wharf and pivoted about the tug; see Fig. 46.

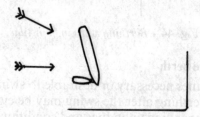

Fig. 46—*Swinging off the berth, one tug, following wind or current.*

When there is a strong head wind or current it is better to give the tug a (good!) stern line and swing the ship stern to the wharf; see Fig. 47.

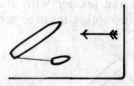

Fig. 47—*Swinging stern to the berth, one tug.*

Lines must be sent ashore aft before the stern swings too far off the berth. It may be necessary to drop an anchor on the bottom to prevent the bow from swinging too fast into the wharf; see Fig. 48.

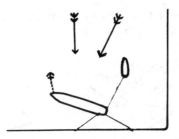

Fig. 48—*Swung off the berth, one tug and an anchor.*

The first preference for the use of two tugs is to place them both alongside; see Fig. 49.

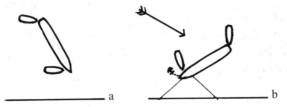

Fig. 49—(*a*) *Swinging with two tugs.* (*b*) *Anchor used to assist berthing.*

The tug aft pushes the ship round. The forward tug initially pulls, to assist with the swing, and later pushes up to prevent the bow of the ship swinging away from the wharf. The anchor can be used to check the bow if there is an onshore wind or current.

If there is a strong head wind or current, or if the tugs are of limited capabilities, the ship is swung stern to the wharf with one tug on a stern line; see Fig. 50.

The forward tug should be secured by its bow, but a single screw tug should also have a line from its stern, to prevent the

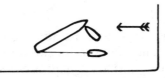

Fig. 50—*Swinging stern to berth with two tugs.*

tug from swinging too far out of position when the ship is
moving astern; see Fig. 51.

Fig. 51 — *Tug using stern line to keep in position.*

A third tug can be given a head line when swinging head
to wharf, or can be secured alongside aft when swinging stern
to wharf. Alternatively it can be given a roving commission:
first to help with the swinging and then to push the ship up to
the wharf; see Fig. 52.

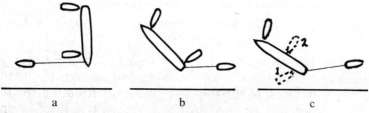

a   b   c

Fig. 52 — (*a*) *Swinging head to wharf with three tugs.* (*b*) *Swing stern
to wharf with three tugs.* (*c*) *Third tug used in two positions* (1 *and* 2).

When four tugs are used it is possible to have one on a line
and one alongside at each end of the ship. This combination
can be varied to suit circumstances during the manoeuvre if
tractor tugs are available with adjustable lines.

Finger berths

The foregoing procedures are adaptable to most berthing
operations, but additional problems arise when berthing
between two "finger" wharves with a cross wind or current,
and with very little space to spare between the wharves.

Figure 53 shows an approach for a vessel berthing at either wharf A or wharf B, with a following wind or current. The approach would be made from further off the ends of the wharves if more space were available, but it must be judged so that the ship is not blown or set past the opening. The ship must pass as close as possible to wharf B, whether berthing at A or B.

At position No. 2 in Fig. 53(a) the fore part of the ship is less affected than the stern by wind or current. The ship must be turned smartly towards berth B, or continue on the same track if berthing at A. Either way, in this illustration, the cut of the propeller when going astern will be favourable for countering set or drift.

An approach from the other direction with a following wind or current would be potentially more dangerous and difficult because the cut would accentuate the ship's swing to starboard; see Fig. 53(b).

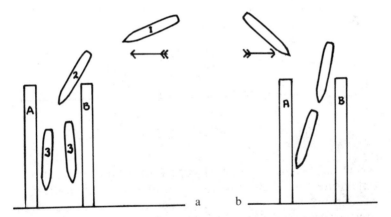

Fig. 53—(a) *Turning to port into finger berths.* (b) *Turning to starboard too late, set onto wharf "B".*

This manoeuvre is a good example of the assertion that a large ship is more difficult to handle than a small ship. Speed of approach must be nicely judged. If the approach is too slow, the ship will be set too far out of position or may collide heavily with the wharf to leeward. A ship that is 100 metres long will take about $2\frac{1}{2}$ minutes to enter the berth at 2 knots. If there were a 2 knot cross current, the berthing could not be attempted at such a slow speed; it would be necessary to approach at 4 or 5 knots. A ship that is 200 metres long will take more time to enter the berth and will require much more distance to be brought to a halt. The speed required to beat the current would make it an unsafe manoeuvre for a large ship.

Tugs should be engaged, to ensure safety when berthing a large ship in these circumstances.

If it is unavoidable that the ship must be berthed without tug assistance, the fore part must be brought alongside first and the rest of the ship driven in while the fore part is kept against the wharf; see Fig. 54.

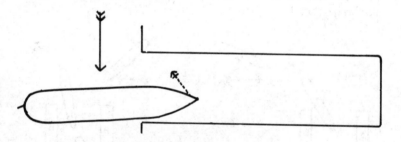

Fig. 54—*Large ship coming alongside forward.*

This procedure can be adopted with wind or current from either direction; but is not advisable in a large ship if the wind or current is strong. Good fendering is required on the landing corner of the wharf. Good head lines must be used and it is essential that they are competently handled by crew and shore linesmen to prevent the ship swinging out of position and causing damage. An anchor should be used to allow better control of the ship's head.

A similar manoeuvre is employed when entering a dry dock or a lock, but anchors cannot be used.

An important difference between a lock and a dry dock is that main engines are used when entering a lock, but cannot be used in a dry dock for fear of dislodging the under-keel blocks. A dock or lock designed to handle large ships usually has adequate line handling facilities. In many cases there is a "training wall", which is an extension of one side of the lock or dock, to enable the ship to be berthed outside and then warped along. Entering a dry dock without a training wall should not be attempted in a large ship without tug assistance if there is a strong cross wind or current.

A ship-handler cannot always choose the direction from which he will approach a berth; but it is advantageous to be heading into the wind or current before turning towards a berth between wharves. A ship can be controlled better this way than when she has a following wind or current. More engine speed can be used without gaining too much speed over the ground. It is possible to compensate for a late turn by taking the way off and allowing the ship to be set back to a more favourable position; see Fig. 55.

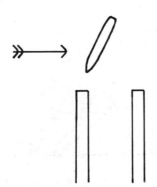

Fig. 55—*Late turn due to over-compensation for wind or current.*

A similar situation arises when passing through a narrow bridge or breakwater opening if it is not possible to make a directly head-on approach; see Fig. 56.

The ship is turned towards the opening with the intention of passing close on the ship's windward side. When approaching from leeward, the turn may be continued beyond the opening; but the turn will be straightened out or reversed on exit if there is a following wind or current. In both cases it is necessary for the stern to be kept up to windward to avoid striking the lee side.

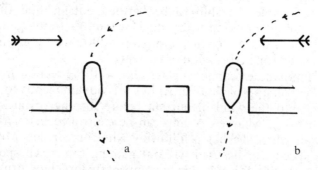

Fig. 56—*Passing through an opening:* (a) *Heading into the wind or current.* (b) *With a following wind or current.*

Departures

With only one tug to assist on departure, the sole tug is used forward; see Fig. 57.

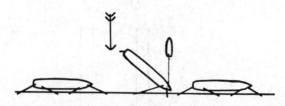

Fig. 57—*Departing with one tug.*

The stern is canted off the wharf by heaving the bow alongside and then going ahead on the engines with rudder hard over towards the wharf. A strong spring must be used forward.

Before letting go the spring, engines are put astern to bring the ship off the berth. The distance that the ship is allowed to travel astern will depend upon the space available. If cramped for room, sternway will be stopped fairly soon, by going ahead with rudder hard over *towards the wharf*. This movement will take the ship's stern away from the wharf and at the same time the tug will pull the bow off so that the ship will move bodily into the channel.

This procedure can be followed whatever the direction of wind or current, but a very wide angle to the wharf is required before letting go if there is a strong wind onto the wharf. The manoeuvre can be assisted by extending the spring along the wharf towards the stern and heaving on this.

A similar manoeuvre may also be used when no tugs are available, but complications arise if there is a head current or a strong onshore wind. An anchor can be dropped after clearing the berth to allow better control of the ship's head; see Fig. 58.

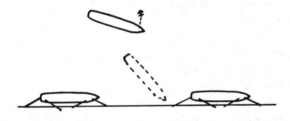

Fig. 58—*Departing without a tug, using an anchor.*

A bulbous bow may prevent the departure from being carried out in this way, because of possible damage to wharf piles. Cranes or gantries on the wharf may also be a deterrent as they are vulnerable to damage when the flare of the bow overhangs the wharf. Such hindrances as these often interfere with an otherwise perfectly sound manoeuvre.

When a ship has to proceed in the opposite direction from that in which she is lying at the berth, it is sometimes possible to pivot the ship by holding her stern against the wharf; see Fig. 59.

Before commencing this manoeuvre it is necessary to be

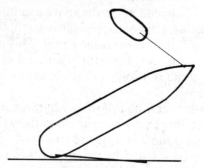

Fig. 59—Swinging with the stern against the wharf.

sure that the construction and shape of ship and wharf are suitable for the ship to be swung without damage. This departure procedure is followed in some river ports without tug assistance when ships are berthed heading upstream. Extreme care is required aft with the spring; when there is a fast current running it is quite a dangerous operation and the consequences could be disastrous if the line parted.

Ingenuity and manhandling of lines can often facilitate the departure of a small ship from an awkward situation; but there are more limitations on what can be done with a large ship. Bigger ships have heavy lines and men are not as willing or able to manhandle heavy lines. Also, the extra mass and momentum of a large ship do not allow the same liberties that may be taken when handling a small ship.

It must sometimes be accepted that a ship cannot be moved from her berth without undue risk to herself and others; it is necessary to wait until more assistance is available or conditions change.

Moving within the harbour

Before berthing, or after departing from the berth, a ship may have to be navigated stern-first for some distance, or may have to negotiate sharp turns from one part of the harbour to another. Tugs are usually placed so that they maintain their same position throughout the manoeuvre; but this is not always possible.

When proceeding stern first, a tug on a towline on each bow is an effective arrangement for controlling the ship. A third tug can be used either on a stern line or alongside aft to counter leeway; see Fig. 60.

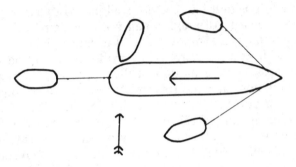

Fig. 60—*Four tug positions, navigating stern first.*

When a ship is proceeding under headway, if tugs are required to assist with the negotiation of bends in the channel or turns in the harbour, they will be more effective alongside.

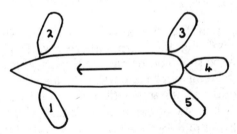

Fig. 61—*Five tug positions for negotiating sharp turns.*

In Fig. 61, suppose the ship has to make a 90 degrees turn to starboard at slow speed.

If there is only one tug to be used, it should be placed forward on the starboard side in position No. 2. As the ship makes her turn, No. 2 tug comes astern; this pulls the ship's bow to starboard, thereby assisting the turn; but it also reduces the ship's forward skidding motion and therefore reduces the turning circle; in addition to this, the tug acts as an anchor and checks headway, so that the ship may be more easily stopped if necessary, or may be given extra engine power to pivot about the tug.

A tug in position No. 1 is not well placed to assist with a turn to starboard. Although it can push the ship in the right direction, there is a component in its pushing which gives the ship more headway, thereby increasing both turning circle and forward skidding motion of the ship; also, the tug is a drag on the port side and this resists the turn to starboard— quite the reverse of the beneficial drag of the tug in position No. 2. Thus it can be seen that there are a number of forces counteracting each other and a tug on the outer side of the turn is only effective if the ship is moving very slowly and the tug is able to operate at a wide angle to the ship's side.

If the ship has to make sharp turns to port and starboard, two tugs secured in positions 1 and 2 provide good assistance, with the inside tug doing most of the work. This combination can also be used when a ship is approaching a berth; the two tugs have an effective braking influence on the ship, and the wharf side tug can be released shortly before arrival at the berth.

Tug No. 4 in Fig. 61 can also assist the ship around corners, by pushing the stern either way. For a turn to starboard, the stern would be pushed to port; this reduces the size of the turning circle and the tug also behaves as an additional rudder. A tug in position No. 3 or 5 would be even better for a turn to starboard or port respectively.

No. 5 tug can pull astern to assist a turn to starboard, but this is not effective unless the ship is almost stopped, because the tug is causing a drag that tries to turn the ship to port.

ACCIDENTS

A manoeuvre which results in damage to the ship or to the wharf is always a reflection on the ship-handler. With hindsight it can usually be shown that the damage would have been avoided *if* the pilot had handled the ship differently. However, there is always more than one cause of an accident. The pilot is dependent upon many other people to ensure the success of a manoeuvre. A message may be misunderstood; a line heaved tight instead of being slacked away; the wheel may be turned the wrong way; an officer or tug master may not give immediate notification of some difficulty that is being experienced. These are all likely contributions towards an accident.

Collisions between ships usually have more complex ramifications than collisions with wharves—fortunately they are rare occurrences. The investigation into a wharf accident may only involve that part of the manoeuvre immediately prior to the impact; but a collision between ships is sure to result in a scrutiny of the whole pilotage. Someone must be blamed, and no one has much chance of coming out unscathed. Ships' officers find themselves more involved than they had expected. Factors which seemed irrelevant take on surprising importance.

A ship's officer will be more able to recall events at a later date if he always takes an involved interest in the handling and progress of his ship. He should be meticulously careful when passing orders and messages and when noting times of events. At all times he must be aware of the ship's course, speed and position; if necessary he can ask the pilot to indicate the ship's position on the chart. A standard procedure is required for testing and checking equipment before arrival and departure. Efficiency and alertness are safeguards against accidents and give a good impression to the investigating authority.

The person presiding over an enquiry is not necessarily well informed on nautical matters and even his expert advisers may be out of touch with modern day practices. The apportionment of blame does not always seem fair or logical—this observation is supported by reversed decisions at subsequent enquiries. The manner in which evidence is presented is as important as the evidence itself. When there are two conflicting stories and neither is convincing, the investigating tribunal may take more notice of impartial—and inexpert—observers; there is always a spectator on the wharf or someone looking out of his harbourside home who sees the whole incident and is willing to become involved.

There is plenty to be learned from accidents. Officers should take every opportunity they can of studying reports, evidence and findings of collision investigations.

A pilot's technique must be tempered by accident prevention procedures. He prefers not to, personally, operate engine telegraph, wheel or whistle. When he gives an order, it is heard by at least one other person, probably by two or three, and it is recorded. An engine movement or even a blast on the whistle may pass unrecognised if there is no verbal order and acknowledgment.

Speed is usually a factor in an accident because the higher the speed the more serious the accident is likely to be. The International Rules for Preventing Collisions at Sea state "Every vessel shall at all times proceed at a safe speed so that she can take proper and effective action to avoid collision and be stopped within a distance appropriate to the prevailing circumstances and conditions." In a congested harbour with numerous small craft, it is sometimes impossible to navigate at a speed which meets this requirement. Consequently, if a pleasure craft capsizes under the bow of a ship and an unavoidable collision occurs, the pilot and the master could be said to have been travelling too fast in the circumstances.

Persons in small vessels do not always appreciate the fact that ships have minimum steerage speeds and restricted draught. Port regulations and the means for enforcing them are necessary to keep adequate, clear navigable water when large ships are being handled.

A harbour pilot is always learning more about ship-handling. Unless he is ultra-conservative, he experiments with variations to his technique. He does not try to be spectacular, but a keen judgment enables him to cut things fine. He prefers to bring a ship neatly alongside by exercising his skills, rather than "berth" the ship 50 metres off the berth and push it up from there by brute force. A master's attitude is slightly different, he is content to see his ship safely alongside with a minimum of excitement, and a "good job" is one that is completed without any damage.

By practice, experience, knowledge and ability a pilot is able to extricate himself and the ship from difficult situations and emergencies. Mechanical faults and breakdowns in communications are common occurrences, but they do not often lead to an accident. Far more accidents are averted than actually happen.

Orders and messages are frequently misunderstood, especially on noisy bridges with language difficulties. Problems of pronunciation and translation are not restricted to discourse between pilot and ship's personnel; a ship's company is often made up of several different nationalities who must find a common language. Some examples of words which are mistaken for each other are "port" and "both"; "full" and "slow"; "ahead" and "astern". "Two" is more distinct than "both" when giving engine orders on a twin screw ship, and "back" is often preferred to "astern". A pilot's orders to tugs can be confused with orders for the ship if the ship's VHF is tuned to the same channel as the pilot's portable radio. Privately operated portable and mobile radio telephones ashore cause interference with messages on board ship, and some irresponsible persons deliberately send false messages.

VHF is used for collision avoidance every day in many ports—usually before a close quarters situation develops. Its success depends upon a perfect understanding between the two parties. Unconventional phraseology should be avoided. Maritime authorities have issued warnings about the dangers of reliance on VHF. Collision Regulations must be complied with.

BRIDGE DESIGN

It is extraordinary that there are hardly two ships with identical bridges, even sister ships. The bridge is the nerve centre of a ship, the seat of command. Why is not more care given to its design? Is a bridge arrangement plan always carefully prepared before a ship is built, or are instruments and indicators fitted haphazardly, with each supplier choosing available space for his own particular piece of equipment?

Pilots, masters and officers are people who can improve ships' bridges, by insisting on minimum standards and supervised installation. In some areas there has to be a compromise between requirements in pilotage waters and requirements on ocean passages. Cost is always a factor, but even unlimited expenditure will not make an ideal bridge unless it is properly planned.

The following are some of the basic essentials:

Visibility

The bridge should be high enough to provide all round visibility with a minimum of interference from deck cargo, cargo gear, deck houses and any other structural features.

Bridge wings

These must extend to the side of the ship, to provide an adequate sighting of the wharf when coming alongside. There must be room for at least two people to stand at the outer end of the wings, and this area must not be obstructed. Side light housing should be on a lower deck and floodlights should be at least below the level of the bridge bulwarks.

Indicators

From any part of the wheel-house or bridge wings it should be possible to see rudder and revolution indicators (and pitch indicators on a vessel fitted with variable pitch propeller).

Large ships should also be fitted with rate of turn indicators and speed indicators.

Wheel-house

Rudder, engine and speed indicators, and compass repeater should be clearly sited in the fore part of the wheel-house, but access to the wheel-house windows must not be obstructed. Non-navigational instruments and consoles should not be situated in the fore part of the bridge.

Noise

Main engines and various noisy auxiliaries interfere with communications within the ship and also make it difficult to hear whistle signals from other vessels. This noise should be muffled as much as possible.

Future improvements

Many organisations are working towards better and more standardised bridges. The International Maritime Pilots' Association has very detailed proposals and the adoption of these would be a major step for safer ship-handling.

THEORY AND PRACTICE

The emphasis in this book has been on *Practical* ship-handling, explained in straightforward terms for practical seamen. A ship-handler has a ship, a harbour, a set of circumstances and a limited supply of practical assistance; his job on each occasion is to apply his own skill and knowledge to these various factors.

Complex formulae for calculating hydrodynamic forces or tug requirements are of no value to the man on the bridge at the time he is engaged in a manoeuvre. Pilots shy away from the pedantic writings of academics and are suspicious of sponsored symposiums and research; they want more depth of water, more space and better tugs, but these improvements are always compromised by cost.

Theory does not always work out in practice. Some small point is often overlooked or under-emphasised. However, pilots, masters and officers should keep abreast of developments. There are many scientists and engineers indirectly involved in ship-handling. Experiments on model ships and model harbours can lead to the construction of more suitable channels, berths and swinging basins and to more efficient rudders, propellers and manoeuvring devices.

No one can become an instant expert by reading a book; certainly not an instant pilot. The possession of a Master's certificate or even a Pilot's licence does not ensure immediate proficiency at practical ship-handling. Among other qualities, a pilot evolves an instinct for doing the right thing at the right time; a little voice inside tells him what he should do next. Manipulating models on a table top or in the water is far removed from handling a real ship.

Wind and current affect ships in different ways and it may seem as though this difference has been over-simplified in the text. It is obviously not possible to explain every conceivable type of manoeuvre and combination of circumstances. Two berths which appear similar may require quite different manoeuvring procedures because of underwater or environmental characteristics. There is always more than one way of berthing a ship or of placing a tug for the same end result; sometimes there is more than one way that is correct. The methods and advice given in this book have been proved by practical experience.

Having studied this book, it is now necessary for the reader to observe its application in every particular situation. An understanding of ship-handling must lead to better ship-handling.

Many of today's officers are pilots of the future and it is never too soon to start learning.

INDEX